C000245639

FOUL DEEDS & SUSPICIOUS DEATHS
IN & AROUND CARDIFF

TRUE CRIME FROM WHARNCLIFFE
Foul Deeds and Suspicious Deaths Series

Barking, Dagenham & Chadwell Heath
Barnet, Finchley and Hendon
Barnsley
Bath
Bedford
Birmingham
Black Country
Blackburn and Hyndburn
Bolton
Bradford
Brighton
Bristol
Cambridge
Carlisle
Chesterfield
Colchester
Cotswolds, The
Coventry
Croydon
Derby
Dublin
Durham
Ealing
Fens, In and Around
Folkstone and Dover
Grimsby
Guernsey
Guildford
Halifax
Hampstead, Holborn and St Pancras
Huddersfield
Hull

Jersey
Leeds
Leicester
Lewisham and Deptford
Liverpool
London's East End
London's West End
Manchester
Mansfield
More Foul Deeds Birmingham
More Foul Deeds Chesterfield
More Foul Deeds Wakefield
Newcastle
Newport
Norfolk
Northampton
Nottingham
Oxfordshire
Pontefract and Castleford
Portsmouth
Rotherham
Scunthorpe
Shrewsbury and Around Shropshire
Southampton
Southend-on-Sea
Staffordshire and The Potteries
Stratford and South Warwickshire
Tees
Uxbridge
Warwickshire
Wigan
York

OTHER TRUE CRIME BOOKS FROM WHARNCLIFFE

A-Z of London Murders, The
A-Z of Yorkshire Murders, The
Black Barnsley
Brighton Crime and Vice 1800-2000
Crafty Crooks and Conmen
Durham Executions
Essex Murders
Executions & Hangings in Newcastle
   and Morpeth
Great Hoaxers, Artful Fakers and
   Cheating Charlatans
Norfolk Mayhem and Murder

Norwich Murders
Plot to Kill Lloyd George
Romford Outrage
Strangeways Hanged
Unsolved Murders in Victorian &
   Edwardian London
Unsolved London Murders
Unsolved Norfolk Murders
Unsolved Yorkshire Murders
Warwickshire's Murderous Women
Yorkshire Hangmen
Yorkshire's Murderous Women

Please contact us via any of the methods below for more information or a catalogue
WHARNCLIFFE BOOKS
47 Church Street, Barnsley, South Yorkshire, S70 2AS
Tel: 01226 734555 • 734222 • Fax: 01226 734438
email: enquiries@pen-and-sword.co.uk
website: www.wharncliffebooks.co.uk

Foul Deeds & Suspicious Deaths In & Around

CARDIFF

MARK ISAACS

Series Editor
Brian Elliott

First published in Great Britain in 2009
and reprinted in this format in 2017 and 2019 by
Pen & Sword TRUE CRIME
An imprint of Pen & Sword Books Ltd
Yorkshire – Philadelphia

Copyright © Mark Isaacs, 2009, 2017, 2019
ISBN: 978 1 84563 084 3

The right of Mark Isaacs to be identified as the Author of this work has been asserted
by him in accordance with the Copyright, Designs and Patents Act 1988.

A CIP catalogue record for this book is available from the British Library

All rights reserved. No part of this book may be reproduced or transmitted in any form
or by any means, electronic or mechanical including photocopying, recording or by
any information storage and retrieval system, without permission from the Publisher in
writing.

Typeset in 11/13pt Palatino by Concept, Huddersfield
Printed and bound in the UK by 4edge Ltd, Essex, SS5 4AD

Pen & Sword Books Limited incorporates the imprints of Atlas, Archaeology,
Aviation, Discovery, Family History, Fiction, History, Maritime, Military, Military
Classics, Politics, Select, Transport, True Crime, Air World, Frontline Publishing, Leo
Cooper, Remember When, Seaforth Publishing, The Praetorian Press, Wharncliffe
Local History, Wharncliffe Transport, Wharncliffe True Crime and White Owl.

For a complete list of Pen & Sword titles please contact
PEN & SWORD BOOKS LIMITED
47 Church Street, Barnsley, South Yorkshire, S70 2AS, England
E-mail: enquiries@pen-and-sword.co.uk • Website: www.pen-and-sword.co.uk
Or
PEN AND SWORD BOOKS
1950 Lawrence Rd, Havertown, PA 19083, USA
E-mail: Uspen-and-sword@casematepublishers.com
Website: www.penandswordbooks.com

Contents

Acknowledgements

This book is dedicated to my beautiful partner in crime Andrea Boyce without whose encouragement I probably would never have taken up this project and who proved to be a source of inspiration and a lovely distraction in equal measure. Thank you darling.

Special thanks to my old friend Marc Saltmarsh, Cardiff's answer to Quincy ME, whose medical knowledge and set of wheels to tour the badlands proved vital.

A big thank you to my colleagues in the Local Studies department of Cardiff Central Library – for their patience – and Brian Lee, a top-notch Cardiffian who pointed me in the right direction for the book. Last but not least thanks to Rupert Harding and Brian Elliott at Pen & Sword Books.

Chapter 1

William McKenzie and the Cardiff Police

Crime and bad lives are a measure of a State's failure – all crime in the end is the crime of the community

H G Wells

The publication of the infamous *Blue Book of Criminal Statistics* in May 1900 succeeded in identifying Glamorgan as the most criminally inclined county in Wales. The propensity for violence and drunkenness were to top its roll call of shame. It is, however, perhaps surprising that its sister authority administered by the Cardiff Borough force was simultaneously (on paper at least) enjoying a remarkable decline in criminal activity. This was no mean feat when one considers that Cardiff was undergoing the most important and industrious period in its history, coping with a population explosion and its dockland Tiger Bay community both celebrated and feared throughout the seafaring world. Chief Superintendent William McKenzie, witnessed the size of Cardiff (and his responsibility) double. A population increase of over 50,000 in 10 years to a then high point of 190,000 is probably woefully underestimated. The extraordinarily transient population of a section of the docklands could never be accurately accounted for. It could well be argued that the reason for this period of social stability during a time of extreme economic and social change was McKenzie's tenure as head of the Cardiff force. As the admiring cult of McKenzie grew, the Watch Committee wasted little time in dubbing him 'half a force in himself'.

This was not to say that the city had become a haven of lawful tranquillity. Far from it. As late as July 1909 Cardiff Borough was vilified by the reformers of *The Humane Review*

Canton Police Station pictured sometime during the late 1880s. Cardiff Public Libraries
Collection

journal as being in the grip of 'flagellomania' – the enthusiastic
deployment of the cat o' nine tails as both a deterrent and a
punishment to those involved in cases of robbery with violence.
At a time when both Merthyr and Swansea had officially
abandoned its use, Cardiff was seen to be overly keen to
dispense its biting swing on *all* sorts of felon. The liberally
inclined *South Wales Daily News* in many ways superseded the
moralising tone of the Tory biased *Western Mail* in its approval
of said punishment. So called *Lists of the Lashed* were published
at regular intervals. In an article dubbed by the *Humane Review*
an 'ecstasy of admiration', the *South Wales Daily News* was to
report: 'Cardiff has its lion's share of hooligans but (flogging)
will eliminate many. The police are MORE than satisfied with
the results of the *cat* punishment.' Despite protestation from all
quarters reaching as far as Home Secretary William Gladstone,
Judge Justice Lawrence, the object of intense scorn for penal
reformers, had that year in Cardiff sentenced seventeen-
year-old Patrick Shannon to twelve months' hard labour and
twelve lashes. All this despite his youth, previous good conduct
and absence of aggravation in the crime. These were indeed

hard times for some in the city. The year 1909 would also see 291 constables on the streets of the city. This was their highest number to date and over double the manpower available to William McKenzie at the start of his tenure as Chief Superintendent.

By the dawn of the twentieth century the Cardiff Borough Police had evolved into one of the most highly regarded and well organised forces outside London. This hard won distinction was the culmination of decades of struggle, graft and guile.

The Cardiff force was originally founded in 1836 under the leadership of the swashbuckling Jeremiah Box Stockdale. It would be his successor, the erudite Scotsman William McKenzie – in many ways his polar opposite – which would succeed in determining the crime fighting force that we still recognise in the city today. Stockdale had been a pioneer and for good or ill truly a man of his time. With his particular exploits and local legend filled with a gung-ho spirit and daring do he none-the-less obtained results. Yet, in Stockdale's day, the majority of men of any quality could far easily find more lucrative employment elsewhere. In one year alone three of his constables were reprimanded for drinking on duty, visiting prostitutes and committing assault – that number was half Stockdale's force! All at the time when it was reckoned that it would take a separate force in itself just to police the brothels of Tiger Bay.

McKenzie would transform the Cardiff police from little more than a backwater posse of local vigilantes and do-gooders in uniform to a crack, model and professional unit in his first twenty years in the job.

McKenzie was born in 1852 in Aberdeenshire. He had grown restless on his father's farm and sought opportunities south of the border. Originally employed by the police in the north of England, by 1876 he had made his home in Bristol. Within three years he had achieved the rank of Inspector and by 1887 Deputy Chief Constable – a quite meteoric rise. Being in the bustling 'capital' of the West Country meant that developments on the other side of the Bristol Channel were common knowledge and the Cardiff force was never far from his thoughts. Applying for their vacancy of Chief Superintedent in

1889, McKenzie would begin his Welsh adventure and usher in an era of modernity and discipline.

Repositioning the Cardiff Force

McKenzie was a realist and recognised that to employ and retain the highest calibre recruits their working conditions and pay must be equal or better than those of comparable forces. Cardiff had long laboured in the shadow of the larger Glamorgan Constabulary. The Glamorgan constables enjoyed higher wages and easier access to advancement than their Cardiff cousins. There was little to deter the best Cardiff men departing the short distance to lucrative pastures new. McKenzie was determined to end this haemorrhaging of talent. The disparity between the neighbouring constabularies was further magnified by the fact that in the closing decade of the 1800's rented accommodation for the Cardiff men was 3 times higher than for the Glamorgan officers despite earning no where near their level of pay.

The 1881 census had illustrated the parlous state of actual police manpower in the Cardiff Borough. The town employed just one constable per 595 head of population making each man responsible for an incredible 53 acres of 'beat'. Compare this to the then similar sized port town of Hull in which although there were 600 head of population for every single constable each would work only 28 acres – almost half that of the Cardiff men. At the same time the relatively huge force of Liverpool boasting some 1,259 men could employ 1 constable per 4 acres – an absolute luxury in policing terms. With the Cardiff police run ragged and physically unable to look after their vast individual patches the town could be viewed as a villains' paradise. The census ten taken years later would see conditions even worse. An angry and frustrated McKenzie would eventually have to cope with allocating just one constable per 900 head of population in the South Wales boom town before being able to turn around the fortunes of the near moribund beast that was the Cardiff Constabulary. Gradual reforms desperately needed to be accelerated for the good of everyone. McKenzie thought long and hard over his new recruitment strategy. His first move seemed contradictory; introducing measures that actually lowered the pay of men joining the force. The carrot for them would be the benefits of remaining with the Cardiff force and a well publicised robust system of annual pay increments for all men was set in place. This would repay loyalty and hard work and encourage recruits to be in it for the long haul. Those not up to scratch would soon fall by the wayside or be dismissed. Special 5 and 10 year service targets would handsomely reward those willing to serve and strive in McKenzie's image.

Promoting through the ranks
McKenzie's promotion of men through the ranks on grounds of bravery, honesty and sheer hard work was a masterstroke. The benefit of such a meritocracy, though now integral to any modern notion of attainment and reward, was something of a radical step during McKenzie's tenure. He had inherited a small force conservative in outlook and labouring under outmoded practice. When identifying the key strand of the constabulary's hierarchy, particular attention was paid to making up Sergeants to acting Superintendents. Identifying potential 'merit class' officers would be similar to today's notion of 'fast-tracking' the brightest and the best. These freshly promoted men instantly enjoyed the respect and camaraderie of their colleagues, thus their deserving of such reward was rarely questioned. If anything it created the impetus among their fellow officers toward greater things and to further their prospects in the town force. It was McKenzie's *raison d'etre* in a nutshell: a competitive, highly motivated team working simultaneously for each other and the common good.

The force certainly needed the enticement of attractive rates of pay and improved working conditions as the life of a Cardiff constable was unquestionably a gritty and extremely dangerous occupation. Those holding the borough's purse strings had little need to dig too deeply to fund McKenzie's pension proposals. Very few men could last the requisite twenty-five years in the job to qualify for a payout in their old age. Long working hours were crippling to both the morale and the health of his men. McKenzie sought to challenge and overturn the received wisdom of the value of continuous 8-hour shifts that left the men exhausted. He advocated splitting the day to allow time for refreshment and recuperation. McKenzie's dynamically fresh proposal was perhaps surprisingly endorsed with enthusiasm by the Watch Committee and would soon pay dividends. An overstretched and fatigued force was little use to the citizens of Cardiff. From at first being allowed just one day off a month, the reforming Chief Constable could now authorise his men one day off a week; the man-hours being made up by the enlisting of two dozen special constables. That McKenzie could facilitate this radical step simultaneously was both pleasing to his men and his paymasters – and stood testament to his policing and organisational genius.

In July 1894, with five years at the helm, McKenzie dropped a bombshell. Drawing acute attention to his importance to the Cardiff force, he informed his employers that he sought a return to Bristol by applying for their vacancy of Chief Constable. He would surely have been the prime candidate. Whether bluff or not (and there is some conjecture) the Watch Committee would be the first to blink, agreeing a pay and accommodation package roughly comparable to the Bristol terms and conditions. Such was his standing at this time it is safe to say that the committee would have fought to retain his services at almost any cost. A deal agreed, McKenzie would stay, but now could never be taken for granted. Five years on, the Scotsman's reputation was at an all time high. On the tenth anniversary of his taking of the post, in 1899, a lavish celebration at the Town Hall witnessed the great and the good of Cardiff queue to heap praise and gifts on their Chief Constable and the allied announcement of a not inconsiderable £100 per annum rise in his pay. This figure exactly mirrored the increase in manpower under his command from 140 in 1889 to 240 in 1899. This could well have been his high water mark. Only two years later a further £100 rise and attractive package of perks was passed despite vociferous protests from Watch Committee members anxious that McKenzie on his gilded pedestal was proving to be too costly an asset.

The cult of McKenzie
For every rise there must be a fall. The year 1902 would become something of an *annus horiblis* for McKenzie. Could it have been an unlucky thirteen years in the job? Figures for the

number of those involved in violent crime, larceny and wounding jumped dramatically. Some reckoned that McKenzie had become complacent. Perhaps for the first time in Cardiff he had found himself out of step with the public opinion he had once ably courted. His vow to close down the majority of public houses in the town was met – not unsurprisingly – with mass hostility. Himself an enigmatic figure, he managed to be simultaneously portrayed in the local press as both a zealous teetotaller *and* a little too fond of the odd tipple. It was true to say that the scourge of drunkenness in Cardiff and his force's inability to contain it over long periods became the chief superintendent's *bete noir*. In retrospect, this may be seen as McKenzie's achilles heel. Although alcohol-induced crime was indeed a serious issue, McKenzie let his own opinions on sobriety and morality cloud his perspective, failing to separate practical policing from what some regarded as the religious dogma attached to his austere, rural upbringing. His stated primary aim to rid the town of this curse left him open to question and ridicule in the papers who were happy to contradict their own view of the man on a day to day basis. The *Western Mail* happily pointed out that neighbouring Newport had more pubs but fewer incidents of drunkenness than Cardiff, and Glamorgan fewer pubs but more violent crime. McKenzie however was not adverse in turn to use the power of the press to his own advantage. It is commonly believed that he had been the author of a series of rather *too* authoritive letters and articles in the *Western Mail* in which their anonymous author spelt out the needs and concerns of the local police and firemen in such a way to astutely garner public sympathy and support.

Prisoner conditions

Those who felt the long arm of the law and the wrath of Cardiff magistrates were not excluded from McKenzie's thoughts. A pragmatist rather than a genuine liberal, he petitioned the powerful Watch Committee as to the abject nature of prisoners' food and conditions while locked in police cells and thus ultimately in his care. Even though the plea would come from their golden boy McKenzie himself this was clearly a step too far for the rather more detached gentlemen of the committee;

William McKenzie Testimonial Fund.

CARDIFF, *6th January*, 1913.

DEAR SIR,

At a largely attended and thoroughly representative meeting of Cardiff Citizens, held in the Grand Jury Room of the Law Courts, on the 18th December, 1912, to consider the recommendations of the Citizens' Provisional Committee as to the desirability of making a public presentation of a testimonial to Mr. WILLIAM MCKENZIE on his retirement from the Head-Constableship of the City of Cardiff after 23 years' service, it was unanimously and enthusiastically resolved to adopt the recommendations, and to make such arrangements as would fittingly commemorate his long and honourable connection with the Police Force.

Letters, warmly approving of the proposals, were read from representative men of all shades of opinion—religious, educational, political and commercial—bearing testimony to the strict impartiality, transparent integrity, and high honour of the retiring " Chief."

The efficiency of our present police force, the comparative freedom of the City from serious crime, and the good order prevailing in our streets, are, in great measure, due to his wise administration and his great ability.

The meeting, convinced that it but expressed the general view held by the Citizens of Cardiff, decided to form itself into Committee, and to open a fund to be called " THE WILLIAM MCKENZIE TESTIMONIAL FUND," and to send out circulars to all the householders of the City, stating the object in view, and inviting those who desired to do so, to send contributions to the Treasurer of the fund. It was felt that services so conspicuous as those rendered by Mr. MCKENZIE should receive public acknowledgment, and you are, therefore, asked to give the proposal your hearty co-operation and support.

The nature of the testimonial will depend on the total amount received, and the time and place of its presentation will be afterwards decided upon, and made public through the medium of the Press.

This appeal is the only one to be issued, and no personal collecting will be done, the Committee considering it best that contributions should be entirely voluntary and sent direct to the Treasurer, Mr. JAMES MILES, 20, The Exchange, The Docks, Cardiff.

As it is particularly desired that the testimonial should be given from every section of the community, even the smallest donation will be greatly appreciated.

Yours faithfully,

PONTYPRIDD, *Chairman of Committee.*

JAMES MILES, *Hon. Treasurer*,
20, THE EXCHANGE, THE DOCKS, CARDIFF.

JOSEPH STANFIELD, *Hon. Secretary*,
LION CHAMBERS,
77, ST. MARY STREET, CARDIFF.

[P.T.O.

A listing of the city's great and good contained in a letter which served as a formal plea to raise funds toward a retirement gift for the outstandingly popular McKenzie. Cardiff Public Libraries Collection

William McKenzie Testimonial Fund.

CITIZENS' COMMITTEE :

Chairman - - The Right Hon. LORD PONTYPRIDD.

The Right Rev. The Lord Bishop of Llandaff.

Lord Ninian Crichton-Stuart, M.P.

Alderman Sir John W. Courtis, J.P.

Sir John Gunn, J.P.

Sir John Duncan, J.P.

Sir W. S. Crossman, J.P.

Principal E. H. Griffiths, Sc.D., Ll.D., F.R.S.

Principal W. Edwards, D.D.

Allgood, Henry G. C. (Agent Cardiff Liberal Association).

Blower, Councillor F. W.

Broad, Dr. B. W.

Cory, Richard, J.P.

David, George

Dawson, Edward

Fisher, Samuel

Griffiths, A. J.

Griffiths, J. Ll.

Henderson, Rev. Alec., B.A.

Hepburn, Professor D., M.D., F.R.S.E.

Heywood, T. M.

Higman, Frank S.

Hughes, Rev. H. M., B.A.

Jones, J. A. (President Coal Freighters' Assoc.).

Joseph, Leo

Jotham, Fredk. H., J.P.

Knapp, W. C. W.

Lewis, W. North (President Chamber of Commerce).

Loveridge, T.

Macintosh, A. C.

Maclean, Donald, M.P.

Maclean, Ewan, M.D., M.R.C.P., F.R.S.E.

McLean, Rev. J. Reynolds

Miles, James

Morgan, W. T. (President Cardiff Football Club)

Morgan, J. Ll. (President Chamber of Trade).

Owen, Evan, J.P. (President Cymmrodorion Society).

Phillips, G.

Pratt, L. H. Allen, LL.B.

Read, H.

Radcliffe, Daniel, J.P.

Rees, Tudor

Samuel, Isaac, J.P.

Seager, W. H.

Stone, Councillor A. J. A.

Smith, Councillor R. J., M.B.

Stanfield, Councillor J., J.P.

Stower, Capt. C. Russell (Agent Cardiff Conservative Association)

Thomas, D. Watkin

Thomas, Rev. J.

Turnbull, Councillor F. H., J.P.

Van den Heuvel, Rev. Father A.

Vachell, C. T., M.D.

Westlake, J. W. (President Licensed Victuallers' Association).

Winks, Rev. W. E.

Williamson, Rev. John, M.A.

Young, William

and to the Chief Superintendent's dismay no funds were forth-coming to make improvements.

These were times of trouble and change in Cardiff. The early years of the 1900s witnessed a period of fractious instability and unrest in police forces across Britain. Chief Constables throughout the land would do well to keep a firm grip on the rudder. A dramatic standoff and threatened strike by an impoverished London Metropolitan police fuelled by bitter rivalry with their more affluent City of London sister force would result in only a meagre pay rise. The repercussions of this dispute were certainly felt in Cardiff by McKenzie and his men. The Scotsman vowed to keep a lid on localised trouble at all costs as commensurate rises were dished out to the country's individual forces. As ever, McKenzie's was the thankless task of serving two masters. He needed to contain the near mutinous anger of his men all the while portraying them as a loyal body worthy of enhanced financial packages to the all important Watch Committee. Of course, McKenzie being McKenzie handled this task with aplomb. His men would abide by a code of good conduct and undertake annual review as to eligibility for increased pay and promotion.

National recognition of McKenzie's tremendous career and achievements was to be finally bestowed in May 1903 with his appointment as the head of the Association of Chief Police Officers. With the type of paradox that marked his tenure he had reached the pinnacle of his career at the same time as a wave of industrial dispute and protest became rife in Cardiff.

McKenzie's legacy is undoubtedly the South Wales Constabulary of the twenty-first century. All his life he had fought to first create then preserve the professional integrity of the police force and create a body of men (and later, women) that was unique in society. A unit with duties that they and only they undertook – their original roster of associated tasks ranged from the sublime to the ridiculous. During his tenure police officers had been called on to be firemen, administer aid to the poor, act as truant officers and even as council food inspectors. McKenzie died on 13 December 1912, aged seventy-three. He had suceeded in defining the role of the twentieth-century constable in Cardiff.

Chapter 2

Thomas Lewis: Hacked to Death by an Irishman Cardiff 1848

The Cardiff of the 1840s was far from the integrated and tolerant society that today we thankfully take for granted. These were not the days of pan-Celtic camaraderie now usually only put to test on the sporting field. The town's first waves of Irish immigrants were viewed with deep suspicion and hostility by the native Welsh both socially and religiously. This ill will would all too often manifest itself in bouts of sporadic violence. It was a generally accepted 'fact' among the Cardiff Welsh that the Irish 'who engaged to work at less rates than the natives have consequently deprived many of employment and driven them to the Union Workhouse'. There was more than a grain of truth in this accusation but the wretchedly poor Irish immigrants had little choice but to either work for pennies or let themselves and their families starve to death. The immigrants were reviled and exploited by bosses and landlords alike. Forced to live in conditions of abject poverty and squalor in criminally overcrowded housing, many succumbed to the dreadful cholera outbreak of 1848, such was the lack of basic sanitation in their dwellings. Under these circumstances the death of a Protestant Welshman at the hands of a Roman Catholic Irishman would be enough to shatter the fragile truce between the nationalities and unleash a shocking fury.

And it would be a grim and inflammatory irony indeed that the killing would be in front of a Catholic church. So serious was

Llansanor Court at the rear of St Mary Street. c. 1889. A vivid example of the squalid living quarters of many of Cardiff's inhabitants. Cardiff Public Libraries Collection

the aftermath of the crime that it would later be acknowledged by many as Cardiff's first (but sadly not last) race riot.

Cardiff on 11 November 1848. Thirty-year-old Thomas Lewis was married with three children and lived in David Street. His father was the landlord of the popular *Red Lion Hotel* situated on the corner of Queen Street and Kingsway and, as such was a familiar face around town. This popularity was a key factor in exacerbating the explosion of anger and outrage surrounding his death. Considering the naked hostility towards the local Irish immigrants in the wake of the murder it is indeed ironic that his father's hostelry had many years previously played host to one of the very first Catholic masses in Cardiff before the advent of the building of the first Catholic church in the town.

The killing

There are almost as many versions of the events leading up to Lewis' death as there were witnesses to the crime. Most accounts, for example, place Lewis at the scene by way of his returning from a boozy wake in Love Lane accompanied by his wife and a friend John Richards. As such, it is quite conceivable that Lewis was drunk and all too eager to taunt and cajole passers by. One newspaper report of his death glosses over this scenario to paint a much more wholesome picture of Lewis simply walking home from working at Crawshay's Wharf. Finishing and paid off at 9.30pm, he had stayed on to assist the unloading of a vessel at Rowan's Wharf. If this was the case it may seem odd that he was accompanied by his wife and baby on his journey home around midnight. One fact generally un-disputed is that Lewis was joined by a small group as he walked the short length of Mary Ann Street towards Whitmore Lane near its junction with Stanley Street where Irishman John Connors stood outside the Catholic church. A rowdy commotion ensued, allegedly instigated by Connors' refusal to step aside to allow Lewis and his associates to pass. Lewis was to confront Connors as 'the leader of troublemakers'. Angry words were exchanged, the verbatim accounts of the dialogue varying so wildly as to be rendered useless as testimony. It was believed that as the initial confrontation died down Lewis turned on his heels and walked away from Connors only to be suddenly struck on the leg by a stone thrown by the Irishman. One account sympathetic to Lewis claims that his wife dropped her baby to the ground such was her fright. This was the catalyst and perhaps the excuse that Lewis needed to once more confront Connors and retaliate. It would prove a dreadful error. Connors ran at the advancing Lewis with a razor-sharp kitchen knife and viciously inflicted deep gaping wounds to the Welshman's face, slicing him from left ear to chin, followed by several mortal blows to his left shoulder and chest. Falling face down, a passing sailor attempted to pull Lewis to his feet and, with the assist-ance of Richards, succeeded in dragging the stricken man to the nearby premises of Dr Evan who pronounced him dead. The later post-mortem would conclude that the deep wound to Lewis' right had 'penetrated the principle artery of the chest, and by causing the blood to flow into its cavities from the heart produced almost instantaneous death'.

The questions and doubt surrounding the fatal attack are legion. Was Lewis actually walking *away* from Connors when he was hit by the stone? Did Connors himself actually chase the Welshman only to stab him to death? Could it have been that

Lewis and Richards *both* chased Connors up the street only to be confronted by the cornered and terrified Irishman? It is almost impossible to answer any of these questions with the remotest degree of certainty. It is however perhaps an interesting fact that during Connors' trial, Lewis' friend Richards claimed to have seen absolutely nothing of the deadly melee despite apparently having been mere yards from the action. Connors was to flee into the darkness and the warren of streets immediately after the stabbing. His pursuers – out run – soon gave up the chase.

Mob rule
The void created by Lewis' death and Connors' disappearance would be swiftly and brutally filled. Mobs of marauding, armed Welsh vigilantes under the pretext of hunting down the fugitive combed the town giving short shrift to Irish families, homes and belongings. It was a timely excuse to teach the immigrants a lesson of just whose hand was on the whip. The Mary Anne/ Stanley Street junction, the epicentre of the Irish community, saw itself under siege with the local police sidelined either by complicity or impotence depending on which account one reads. Starting in the evening of 12 November, a virtual state of anarchy would grip the town for seven days and seven nights. It is worth noting that at this time Cardiff could boast only a dozen full-time police officers, a number nowhere near sufficient to effectively serve the burgeoning town.

The killing was not without recent precedent. At this time violent confrontation between Welsh and Irish was never more than one sideways glance or cross word away. Only on 8 May a group of Welsh labourers had assembled at a cottage on the outskirts of Swansea for a drunken party in honour of a local couple about to marry. With the drink flowing and spirits high the group were later joined by a band of Irish railway navvies who had been working nearby. After first welcoming the new-comers the party atmosphere would soon turn sour. A heated dispute broke out between a Welshman and one of the Irish over the low wages that the navvies had consented to; a constant and bitter cause of resentment to the native population. The inevitable fist fight would leave two Welshmen, John Williams and Jenkin Evan, both dead from stab wounds to the heart. Their assailants managed to flee as far as Cardiff but were soon apprehended. As ever the truth behind the killings was a cause of great dispute. A not uncertain degree of innate prejudice would see Irishmen Thomas Martin and Michael Leary face the gallows for their part in the crime.

The inquest commenced at Cardiff Town Hall at lunchtime on the Monday following Lewis' death. Presided over by the district coroner, R L Reece, it made slow progress. Having sat for six hours it was decided that proceedings would be adjourned until the Thursday 'to give time for apprehension of the murderer'. This postponement was significant and a worrying indication that police enquiries were not at all going to plan. Connors would later claim that all the while the authorities fretted and recriminated he was still hiding out in Cardiff right under their very noses – a boastful jibe at the detectives' apparent inefficiency. It would be a far from ridiculous claim. Such were the horrifically overcrowded rooms of the Irish lodging houses the task of prizing out one man from the bosom of Cardiff's Irish enclave would be a massive test of police resolve.

Newspapers

The formidable Superintendent Jeremiah Stockdale, head of the Cardiff force, was not immune to the criticism of the seemingly inept way he had handled the pursuit for Connors that allowed the killer to be at large for a week after the crime. Stockdale himself had been on duty at the nearby Hayes as Lewis was done to death but arrived at the scene too late to collar the wily Connors. With the anti-Irish feeling running dangerously high in the town Stockdale would be pilloried in the press and put up as a scapegoat for the authorities' perceived inability to keep the rowdy, lawless immigrants in check.

Even in the 1840s local newspapers were of vital significance in both the shaping and distorting of the 'truth' of Lewis's murder and its aftermath. The press (and in particular the *Cardiff & Merthyr Guardian*) were complicit and fairly at ease in whipping up a feeling of prejudice and hostility towards the Irish. Literate yet quite biased editorials often plunged into purple prose and rhetoric, feeding the anger and untutored minds of the resident Welsh-born Cardiffians who sought reason and excuse to wreak a punishment on their unwelcome guests.

A private letter from an unknown source gives a fascinating if less than accurate appraisal of the tumult in the town. First published in the *Cambrian* newspaper and later reprinted in *The Times* of 20 November 1848, it would depict Cardiff on the brink of a virtual civil war: 'We are in a state of commotion here ... [a Welshman] was murdered by an Irishman, which has caused a strong feeling against all Irish. Last night they broke the windows of the Romish chapel and the priest's house. The priest has left town today fearing for his personal safety, the feeling against him is great; some people have taken it into their heads he had harboured the murderer.'

The letter goes on to give detail of the way that all manner of Irish workers in the town were discharged from their duties: 'There was not an Irishman employed in the town or neighbourhood on Tuesday.' Quite ominously, the correspondence concludes with an opinion as to a conclusion to the unrest: 'At all events this will not end without a display of much ill feeling. It is a most unprovoked affair and very horrible.'

The anonymous letter appeared well informed and cleverly managed to convey a pro-Welsh 'us and them' scenario without pandering to naked religious bigotry. It was particularly detailed in regard to the deceased's life and times – information not necessarily in the public domain. With the concept of 'public relations' and 'spin' a century away, it was not unknown for the most senior police officers to pen anonymous letters to the local papers as a vehicle by which to vent their spleen and put on record 'their' version of contemporary events. Perhaps even Superintendent Stockdale himself.

As *The Times* of 16 November succinctly put it: 'On Monday evening the excited and exasperated populace attacked the dwellings of the Irish, broke their windows, burst open their doors, and burnt some of their furniture, and had it not been for the interference of the police, a serious riot would have been the consequence. They also attacked the Catholic chapel, demolished the windows and did considerable damage to the priest's house.'

With regard to the great antipathy toward the Irish it continued: 'On every occasion that an opportunity is afforded this [hostility] breaks out with great violence, and demands the [participation] of the civil authorities to quell it.'

The funeral

Lewis' funeral would be something of a grotesque spectacle and show of strength by both factions. In fear of savage reprisals metered out on their fellow countrymen, large groups of Irish navvies from all over South Wales descended on the town armed with pick axes. They in turn would be met by a travelling posse of Welshmen from Merthyr intent on just such violent interaction. Chaotic scenes developed along the route of the cortege from St John's church to the cemetery in Adamsdown as onlookers jostled to view the coffin and vocalise their feeling of outrage. Special constables were hastily sworn-in in an attempt to keep the intense feeling of antagonism from boiling over in to pitched battle. It is to their credit that the emotionally charged day passed off with the minimum of incident.

Back of St Mary Street and the Taff before it was later diverted. St John's church is seen on the left. Cardiff Public Libraries Collection

The trial

Although a then substantial reward of £50 was put up for information leading to the apprehension of the killer it appeared that dogged police enquiries would succeed in running Connors to ground. After a trail of false information and rumour, strongly indicating that Connors had fled home to his native Ireland, the fugitive was eventually tracked down to an over-crowded boarding house in the town of Pontypridd. When challenged by Police Superintendent Thomas, the Irishman displayed little of the guile and hubris that had kept him at large for a week. Rather half-heartedly giving constables a false name, he made little attempt to resist his escort back to Cardiff, to face the full wrath of the law and the violent derision of the gathered Welsh mobs.

Connors was committed for trial at the Glamorgan Assizes held in Swansea on 27 February 1849. The accused went without legal representation and relied on portraying himself as an honest, hardworking man who had only set upon Lewis with a blade in retaliation for being manhandled by the Welshman. During the trial unsubstantiated rumours abounded as to Connors having once killed a man in Ireland which served to further blacken his name. A handful of witnesses were called who did much to corroborate the Irishman's version of events. The doubt thus cast in the jury's mind as to exactly who attacked whom would prove crucial for Connors. The assize judge, William Erle, made it abundantly clear to them that the Irishman should only face the gallows if they were certain that Connors' actions were of a truly murderous intent. To the considerable chagrin of Benjamin Matthews the prosecution attorney, the jury found Connors guilty of the lesser charge of manslaughter – not a capital offence. The decision had been close indeed with the Judge himself expressing the view that in his opinion the line between the two crimes may well have been crossed. Connor would be 'lucky'; transportation on a filthy, sweltering convict ship would be his punishment. He would live out his days in the Australian penal colony at Botany Bay.

As was common in such cases, the jury donated their court fees to a fund that would alleviate the immediate financial burden on Lewis' widow and children and keep them away from the poor house.

It would be far too trite to claim that the slaying in Stanley Street was the final push towards harmonious relations and the healing of the rift between Catholics and Protestants in Cardiff. It was not. The enmity between the faiths would remain for many years to come in the face of a greatly increased number of Catholics residing in the town and the subsequent establishment of a network of dedicated schools and churches to cater for them. It has been said that it was only the advent of the Marquess of Bute's conversion to Roman Catholicism and his omnipotent position among the great and the good of Cardiff that would finally set the seal of approval and acceptance of the Catholic faith among the population in general.

Chapter 3

Honora Dutch: Killed by Her Enraged Husband Canton 1865

Tragedy and comedy are strange bedfellows in this a tale of what was, at least geographically, the 'Wild West' of Cardiff. It concerns the exploits of a drunk, a brawler and a donkey. But, unlike the musical hall joke that the image conjures up, here a violent killing remains long after the laughter ceases.

November 1865. John and Honora Dutch were a well known married couple in Canton which was merely then a hamlet in close proximity to the town of Cardiff. Their rumbustiousness and somewhat volatile relationship preceded them. With their incessant quarrelling and fighting not for nothing was Mrs Dutch known locally as 'Black Eye'. Her husband, John, though nearly sixty years old was a powerful, well-built man regarded as hardworking but possessed of a permanent scowl. His wife's temper was quite considerably worse than his own and she, unlike her husband, was all too fond of the demon drink. Their miserable Punch and Judy-like existence was compounded by their impecuniousness and having no less than three handicapped children to support. In their cramped two-room dwelling times were indeed harsh for the Dutch family.

To supplement his meagre income as a labourer for a wealthy Llandaff contractor, John Dutch and his older sons kept a donkey with which they fetched and carried for local tradesmen. The poor beast often lay tethered in the filthy lane and yard which served as a communal entrance to their tenement

Llandaff Road. The red brick apartments at the right of the picture occupy roughly the site of the dwelling in which Honora Dutch lived during the 1860s. To the left is the Butchers Arms *public house which would have then been familiar to Dutch as the* Market Tavern. The author

nestled in a row of at least outwardly respectable houses on the southern end of Llandaff Road – opposite the *Market Tavern* (later known as the *Butcher's Arms*). With at least eight other families living cheek by jowl the block was well known to the local constabulary.

On Saturday 25 November, as was common practice, the donkey was released into the street to enjoy a free meal of the neighbours' hedgerows. Unfortunately for the blighted family Dutch on this occasion one householder took great exception to this al fresco dining and had the donkey impounded. This seemingly insignificant comic incident would ultimately lead to the painful, bloody and untimely death of the indomitable Honora Dutch.

The cost of keeping the animal had long been a cause of strife between Mr and Mrs Dutch and, with John dutifully paying the 4s 8d to secure its release the following Monday, Honora was incensed. Returning to their home around 6pm, he was greeted with a tirade of venomous abuse about his 'foolish timorousness', prompted by her assertion that too much money had been needlessly handed over to regain the donkey. A bitter quarrel over the course of half an hour degenerated into a full-scale brawl with John punching his loquacious wife clean off her chair and onto the lap of Mary Sullivan their lodger.

Honora's litany of curses did not diminish even when sprawled on the staircase while being kicked and beaten with the back of the now broken chair. This frenzied scene was played out in near complete darkness as the kitchen's solitary candle had long since been knocked over and extinguished. Struggling for breath but still calling her husband some 'foul names' Honora seized her chance and rushed to the back door to escape pausing only to hurl a serving plate at her husband's head. What had seemed to John Dutch as the conclusion of their dispute was actually only his wife taking time to re-arm herself. A handful of the yard's mud and excrement was aimed through the door, straight at her now seated husband. The slapstick nature of this tawdry battle of wills would now give way to an altogether more brutal scenario.

Attracted by the commotion, a gaggle of near neighbours witnessed Mrs Dutch pursued by her furious husband into the yard only to be dragged back by an outstretched arm. Crying out 'Dutch, for shame – please don't kill me!' her indignation had now turned to terror. A sickening blow to the stomach with a clenched fist stopped her in her tracks. Stumbling near the yard's linen-post, Honora fell across a small metal wash tub. In this prone position she was near defenceless. In a blind rage her husband weighed in with a rain of blows to her head and vicious kicks to her back and abdomen. Despite pleas from the assembled onlookers, Dutch's heavy hobnailed boots continued to exact a merciless revenge on his wife's prostrate body until it seemed that even he thought enough was enough and backed away.

With her attacker retreating inside, a neighbour carried the dying Mrs Dutch next door for help. By the time the district surgeon, Mr Pearse, arrived Honora Dutch was dead. On initial examination her body proved a litany of small cuts and old bruises. A short while later that evening, around 7.30pm, PC

Williams in attendance located John Dutch in his shed and promptly arrested him on suspicion of the wilful murder of his wife. With so many witnesses it would appear an open and shut case but Honora would become a victim not only of John but her own reputation.

Honora's husband freely admitted her killing. His deadpan logic betrayed little in the way of remorse. With a world weary shrug he said: 'I suppose I killed her, she is dead now'. The prisoner would be less forthcoming as to the brutality of his actions. Having been 'black-guarded' about the donkey, the 'several clips' to her head were in reality un-pulled punches and the 'two kicks with [his] shoe' at least a dozen blows delivered with heavy duty working boots.

Secretly, the police must have been glad to see the back of poor old Honora Dutch. She had been arrested half a dozen times and had spent short spells in prison. At least while incarcerated they had enjoyed brief respite from calling at Llandaff Road to intervene in her violent altercations with her husband. With regard to the victim, the local constable agreed, with perhaps a little understatement, that 'when she was vexed she was vexed'; and while conceding that John Dutch was a 'very steady man', the deceased was of 'an aggravating disposition'.

During the initial inquest held at the nearby *Canton Hotel*, district coroner R L Reece stated his belief that none of the blows to the victim's head or torso were sufficient to precipitate her death. Similarly, it was his opinion that even though she had been kicked repeatedly in the stomach it was the fall against the wash tub that had likely caused the 'rupture of her spleen and fatal haemorrhage' – its profusion such that it took less than ten minutes for her to bleed to death. The clear implication was that John Dutch had perhaps *hastened* his wife's demise but not directly caused it. The whisper was everywhere – she *had* been a hopeless alcoholic after all.

Did John Dutch get away with murder by virtue of his wife's unsavoury character? Whatever the case, it would be the findings of surgeon Pearce that would save John Dutch from the gallows. During the Llandaff Petty Sessions, held on 4 December 1865, the results of a thorough autopsy would show that although most of Honora's vital organs were reasonably healthy her liver was in an 'unusually diseased state' due to years of ravage by alcohol. Pearce reckoned that such was the liver's parlous condition its fragility would mean that her life expectancy could possibly have been mere weeks – irrespective of any assault. The inquiry would pivot on these findings. With clear uncertainty as to whether it was the fall against the tub or the blows delivered by the accused that had fatally ruptured the woman's spleen the magistrates recommended that: '[Having] gone carefully through the whole of the evidence and although the capital offence was done away with [the prisoner] should take his trial at the next assizes for manslaughter'.

Even facing a long period of hard labour, John Dutch could count himself fortunate – men had certainly swung for less. With neither Mr nor Mrs Dutch now in residence, perhaps the more law-abiding folk in that troubled part of Canton could now finally get some peace.

Chapter 4

Foul Deeds in Cardiff Docks 1869

Cardiff Docks in the late 1860s. The port's growth and attendant increase in economic activity was breathtakingly rapid. In little more than a generation the town had transformed itself from no more than a fishing village into a boomtown – a Welsh Klondike. Cardiff coal was king and those hungry enough travelled from the four corners of the globe for a slice of the economic pie. Cardiff was on its way to becoming – for a period – the most important seaport in the world. Nothing typified the town more than its docklands. By the close of the decade and into the early years of the 1870s, Butetown and Tiger Bay had taken on much of the character (both human and physical) that would make their locale both celebrated and notorious in equal measure.

The sheer toughness and brutality of life at sea was brought ashore each and every day at Cardiff Docks. Sailors and dockers lived on their wits – and by and large their own rules – irrespective of the local constabulary. The camaraderie felt by seafarers operating from an international port, though real, was easily strained when times were hard and the drink had flowed. These divisions were all too often along lines of race and nationality. Scores were settled without compunction and the opportunity to exact violent revenge all too tempting a prospect. Probably no other section of society had the opportunity to commit a serious crime and disappear out in to the wide ocean before an alarm could be raised. At this hectic international port the fragile 'melting pot' could and would become a powder keg in the blink of an eye. It's worth remembering at this time the local constabulary patrolling the docks would readily return

Bute East Dock, c.1890. Cardiff Public Libraries Collection

to their station to retrieve their cutlasses as and when the need arose – as it often did. Those apprehended by the police, described rather quaintly as fighting in a 'tipsy frenzy', would encounter the full wrath of the law.

The sailors were hard-working men leading hard-drinking lives. I'm sure that some of their lady folk were not too far behind. Many a wild night was enjoyed by the international clientele of the bars and dives of Tiger Bay. Life in the close confines of sailing vessels and cheap rooming houses were a breeding ground for crime and violence fuelled by alcohol. In this Cardiff dockland underworld of crooks, pimps, prostitutes and thugs the scourge of the knife was endemic; and later the year 1869 would be viewed as something of a low water mark in crime fighting.

Thomas Williams

July in 1869. What shall we do with the drunken sailor? Thomas Williams was to suffer the fate of many a seaman, worse for wear from alcohol, returning home from a heavy night's drinking in Tiger Bay. The apprentice pilot would have done well to heed advice about walking home alone late at night. An inebriated man was an easy prey for the thieves and wharf rats that haunted the back alleys around the docks, all too ready to relieve the unwary of their pay. The lucky were merely rolled for their cash, some beaten and even their clothing stolen. Others would end up in the 'Ditch', or the Glamorganshire Canal, their lifeless bodies dredged out by police. Williams may well just have been in the wrong place at the wrong time. Around midnight on 17 July he had left the *Rothesay Castle* pub on Bute Street in whose saloon bar he had been 'drinking hard' for three days. He soon found his path blocked by two men walking in the opposite direction. The lane was quite narrow so he pushed between the two, believing their intention was robbery or worse. The pair did not yield and blows were exchanged, the fracas quickly attracting further combatants. A witness would later tell that one of the original pair then brandished a knife which 'glittered in his hand'. It was to be used with deadly force. A sickening wound was inflicted upon Williams' belly, the blade opening up his abdomen. Welshman Williams dropped to the cobbles like a stone.

As his assailants fled they were to run almost directly into a group of policeman whose presence was never too far away on Saturday night patrols of this lawless den of vice. Brought before the Borough magistrates, they were identified as Italian sailors named Gallono and Pietro Gastro, from the ship *The Santo Chireco*. They were doomed. Witnesses were plenty and a number swore that it was Gallono Gastro who had wielded the murderous blade; indeed the dagger found at the scene was positively identified as his property. Their victim had clung onto life for over six hours, finally breathing his last around 6am. Not even the close proximity of the attack to the nearby hospital ship was enough to prevent his bleeding to death. Before he died, Thomas tearfully expressed his wish to the attendant surgeon that he would soon be in heaven. He was nineteen years old.

Amongst the braying crowd there was one dissenting voice. Whilst formally identifying Gallono and Pietro as being part of the violent melee, one witness was absolutely adamant that neither was the killer. He was convinced that there was a third man in the alley confronting Williams who was never apprehended by police. It was he that had cruelly stabbed the drunken apprentice. With their relatively poor grasp of English, the Italian prisoners could do little to convince the authorities of their professed innocence. Despite the intervention of the Italian Consul both of the sailors were committed for trial at the Glamorgan assizes on a charge of wilful murder.

Crimping

The unwary had real need to beware. In a practice known as 'crimping' it was not unknown for unscrupulous shipmasters to comb the sleazy boarding houses of Tiger Bay to supplement their crew numbers by violent coercion and kidnap. Even those sailors legitimately seeking a berth had need to be vigilant. With white European seamen by custom selected for signing on first, the remaining places for deckhands could be ten times over-subscribed. The 'coloured' or black seaman came much lower down the employment pecking order. It was said that those left jobless at the back of the queue were not averse to using a knife to stab a successful black candidate to prevent him from taking up his awarded post.

Andreas Ohlsen

Cardiff in early August 1869. To those who knew seaman Andreas Ohlsen he was a quiet and resourceful man. Like many of the foreign nationals frequenting the bustling port of Cardiff at this time he was Scandinavian, born and raised in the Norwegian town of Bergen. Such were the number of his compatriots living and working around the docks that a distinctly 'Norwegian' church had been constructed in the area the previous year to solely cater for their spiritual needs. Perhaps the most famous of Norway's transplanted community would be the internationally acclaimed author Roald Dahl, born in Cardiff and himself baptised in its Norwegian church in 1916.

As a sailor Ohlsen had plied his trade under the watch of Captain C Wulf (Sea Wolf!) on a Norwegian registered vessel named *The Norcap*. It had first set sail in the spring of 1867 carrying immigrants from Bergen to a new life in the Canadian wastelands. The vessel was a 'bark' (or 'barque') so named as to its peculiar method of rigging. This was important as triple-masted craft rigged in such a way could be operated by far fewer crew members than an ordinary ship. This was cost effective but there was a price to be paid elsewhere. Andreas Ohlsen would soon know the consequences of this cheek by jowl existence of overworked men in close confines.

Norwegian vessels were frequent visitors to Cardiff waters often laden with a valuable cargo of timber – a much prized commodity from the Baltic. On this occasion *The Nordcap* had docked at the Welsh port to collect a consignment of that nation's prized export – coal. The vessel had rested in the Bute East Dock for some two weeks since its arrival from Liverpool, its previous landing-place. The men on board were glad of some respite from the harsh life at sea, the relations amongst the crew having been far from harmonious to say the very least.

The crew were virtually Norwegians to a man. The ship's steward, William Byron, was very much the exception and an outsider. Born on the Cape Verde island of Sao ('St') Vincent off the West African coast, he was distrusted by his colleagues – a feeling reciprocated by the young black sailor. The highly volatile atmosphere on board *The Nordcap* would soon explode. All agreed that Ohlsen had been on the most unfortunate terms with Byron for some time, the young steward joining the vessel when it docked in his native Cape Verde some fourteen months earlier. During the meagre supper on board on the evening of 19 August 1869 this mutual animosity would turn deadly.

The truth of the matter one shall never know but Ohlsen berated Byron for the foul coffee that he had served him, swearing that that the steward had intentionally contaminated his drink. Never slow to react, Byron was on his accuser in an instant. Tables and crockery crashed around the tiny galley in which the crew took their meals. As the two scuffled on the floor the blade of a knife flashed in the candlelight. This was indeed the weapon of choice amongst the sea dogs frequenting Cardiff's least salubrious taverns and back alleys, often being used to 'settle' disagreements. Byron would claim that Ohlsen had dealt the first blow before dropping the kitchen knife to the floor. His arm slashed, the Cape Verdian lunged to retrieve the weapon and in one lethal action forcibly pushed the blade into Ohlsen's chest 'penetrating the heart and causing almost instantaneous death'.

The wooden floor was awash with blood when Byron was dragged off his victim by his fellow crew members and placed in the custody of the police. In his defence Byron claimed that he had acted merely to protect himself and feared that the other crew members would kill him. With the barbaric slaying of the Norwegian in plain view of his fellow countrymen, his fears may not have been unfounded. The crew were to testify that they witnessed Byron surreptitiously cutting *himself* after the fight to feign prior injury and thus claim self defence. He was perhaps lucky that his fate was in the hands of the magistrate rather than the arbitrary justice and retribution metered out in an instant by hardened sailors. His luck was to be fleeting. The young sailor would face the gallows, possibly a victim of both racial prejudice and the word of the mob.

By any measure it had been a violent and bloody year in the town. With the nearby island of Flat Holm being fortified in fear of immanent French invasion, the local press found its attention drawn to strained foreign relations closer to home. On 20 August, under the headline 'Another fatal case of stabbing in Cardiff', the *Western Mail* would lament: 'The unenviable notoriety for stabbing which Cardiff enjoys does not seem likely to subside.' After listing a catalogue of recent crimes the editorial concluded (seemingly oblivious to its Welsh location) thus:

> *It is a consolation, if a poor one, to know that these malignant acts are invariably perpetrated by foreigners, Englishmen as a rule not resorting to the dastardly practice using knives.*
>
> *It seems to be an ineradicable vice of a sailor to use his knife in his quarrels. This remark is especially true in its reference to the foreign sailor, who whether in his cupa [sic] or not, has always shown a too fatal readiness to produce his knife as an effective means of retaliation or aggression. Wherever there is a seaport, the police records only too truly demonstrate that lamentable fact.*
>
> *[It is] necessary, in order to check this evil, to pass exceptionally heavy sentences in these cases. It is to be regretted that recently there has been too much evidence of a growing fondness for the*

knife on the part of the sea-faring class in Cardiff and the district. The prevalence of such cases here was made the subject of reference by the learned chairman of quarter sessions in his last charge to the grand jury.

Chapter 5

PC William Perry: Knifed by a Butcher
Westgate Hotel
1872

The Cardiff of the late nineteenth century was a place where a man could shake off the past and create himself anew. The town had begun to sprawl and its population explode – a magnet drawing every race, colour and creed from within the British Isles and without to settle and make a living. Such an influx would bring with it a degree of anonymity useful to those wishing to make a fresh start whether in matters of the heart or of business or both.

One such migrant was butcher's apprentice John Jones who had arrived in Cardiff from Wolverhampton accompanied by his wife in the late 1860s. They had not always been such. In their Black Country home town they had been Benjamin Swann, a slaughterman and his 'spouse' Ann, Mrs Hollingsworth – the wife of his employer. When he fled Wolverhampton the now 'Mr Jones' took with him more than just a set of knives. The runaway lovers in the guise of the respectable Mr & Mrs Jones would soon establish a reasonably successful pork butcher's shop in Wharton Street above which they lived. In time the industrious Jones would also set up a stall in the nearby Canton Market which also provided premises for the slaughter of the beasts. Neither business thrived but together provided a degree of financial stability that kept the couple afloat.

Illness and madness
Whereas Jones would find it relatively easy to bury his former persona he could do little to shed the baggage of his mental

frailty. He arrived as he had left; a man given to the blackest of moods and susceptible to severe bouts of depression. The couple's 'honeymoon' period over Jones would find himself ill-equipped to reconcile their efforts towards a new life with a grotesquely heightened fear of financial failure. Hampered by his obsession with his social standing in the local business community, Jones' increasing alcoholism did little to salve his troubled mind. In time spirits and self doubt would prove a potent and destructive brew.

Those close to Jones certainly believed that it was his love of the bottle that had instigated his monetary woes, with working days lost, incapacitated by stupor. As his mental health deteriorated the one problem certainly fed the other. It was true that the butcher had cash flow problems but probably nowhere near as calamitous as those he saw magnified and distorted through the bottom of a glass.

Convinced that fellow local butchers Jeffries & Ayres were plotting to ruin him, Jones' damaged psyche vacillated between manic bravado and crippling paranoia, with neither condition conducive to coping with his daily life. He irrationally feared not only the unlikely prospect of his creditors forcing him in to debtor's prison but also the tavern gossip that circulated amongst Cardiff's tradesmen as to his increasingly financially embarrassed state. His wife would later refute these accusations claiming that her husband was solvent; borrowing nothing and owing no one but a very real £51 being owed by her husband to Fligenstone the Canton pawnbroker gave lie to this belief.

His business sense impaired by his growing addiction, he would gain a reputation for eccentric behaviour around the hostelries and markets for needlessly giving away his belongings – acts prompted more surely by intoxication than altruism. The line that separates the cheery reveller and the chronic alcoholic is thin at best but it is believed that during the winter months of 1872 Jones, acutely aware of his predicament, was embarking on a period of self imposed abstinence.

Sadly John Jones' descent into insanity would progress unabated by the love of his wife and his attempts to reform. A recent visit to the Victoria Rooms in St Mary Street, for an evening's musical entertainment, strayed far from the hour of respite that had been planned. As the night wore on an increasingly agitated Jones' asserted that the performer on stage was 'singing against him'. Convinced that each and every lyric was a personal defamation of his character, he could bare it no longer and his wife struggled hard to placate the tormented man. Now with a different vocalist taking centre stage a change of repertoire brought little consolation. This was the final straw for Ann. As the curtain went down she led Jones awkwardly from the stalls all the while ranting and raving at the still seated audience whom he felt were in collusion with those who mocked him from the wings.

This tragi-comic scene was echoed some months later at the theatre when the guileless ribaldry of a pantomime story was interpreted by Jones as a criticism of him and nothing less than the very story of his life. The downward spiral of his paranoid delusions was almost at its shocking conclusion.

30 December 1872. The night before the killing of Perry would be as horrid and frightening as any the couple had experienced. Ann Jones has frequently been locked in a room by a neighbour to protect her from her husband's violent impulses. The eve of the New Year would find Jones a desperate mentally broken man. His wife would later explain that: 'For some days previous [to the killing] he appeared very odd in his manner and made use of some very queer expressions.' This was certainly evidenced by his waking terrified during the small hours of the New Year's Eve. Leaping from their bed and tearing the shirt from his body, Jones dashed downstairs into his commercial premises. Screaming 'They are in the shop now!' the butcher inexplicably set about smashing his window display of produce. The spectral 'they' of his fears would never be identified. Returning to the bedroom calmed by a sleeping draught he would be roused an hour later by the sound of a distant whistle which he mistook for a fire engine. Again he would hurl himself from his bed, this time convinced that they would be washed out of their home. Ordering his wife to don every item of clothing she possessed as a precaution an exhausted and tormented Jones would finally drift off into sleep.

Waking at 6am, Ann would find her husband in remarkably good spirits; a marked contrast with the previous night's terrors.

Although puzzled by Jones' needless instruction to light the fire under the boiler, she complied, happy to see him in a more positive frame of mind. With preparations to make for the following week's trading Jones left their shop at 8am for the short walk to Canton market. Smiling as he waved goodbye, he promised to return within the hour. Having suffered the years of soul searching and heartache that followed their elopement and bogus marriage, this would be the last time that poor Ann Jones would see her 'husband' alive.

The crime

For a man with a reputation as a drunk only one man would give evidence to suggest that Jones was intoxicated that morning on his travels to Canton and back. In fact, when inviting Thomas Thornton to join him for a warming dram in the *Canton Cross Brewery* Jones only partook of a peppermint cordial while his companion enjoyed a whisky. Thornton was a retired police inspector and long time associate of Jones who had found work in his old age tending to the boilers in Canton market. Jones

The Canton Cross Vaults. *John Jones was to share a Christmas drink here with his associate Thomas Thornton on the morning of PC Perry's murder.* The author

had travelled there to meet him that morning to seek his assistance in slaughtering some pigs later in the week. Their last meeting had been marred by the butcher's agitation over a debt of £5 that he had sought but failed to repay his friend. But this morning Jones appeared affable enough as Thornton witnessed his friend secrete one of his slaughtering knives into his coat pocket before they walked the short distance to the hostelry. It would be the first key to that day's impending tragedy.

The second would be the sighting of PC William Perry along the Cowbridge Road. Seeing the constable passing the work-house gate Jones, now alone, hollered to Perry to join him in the adjacent *Wyndham Inn* for a drink. The butcher was clearly in convivial mood. The two men were known to each other and, although never on the best of terms, Perry declined the invitation graciously but offered Jones festive greetings. Jones was not a man apt to take no for an answer and, his ego some-what bruised, briskly pursued the constable, drawing close to him near Treseder's nursery gardens. Witnesses would remark that the two men strolled side by side in amicable conversation pausing even to exchange compliments of the season with passers by. Jones was overheard to be explaining to Perry that he planned soon to leave Cardiff for Carmarthenshire or Pembrokeshire once he had resolved some outstanding business matters.

Observed by the Toll Keeper William Evans, the unlikely pair approached the corner of Cathedral Road and the Westgate Turnpike in good humour but something unknown yet highly significant occurred between the two men that would darken the mood greatly. Halting at the lamp post, Jones turned to Perry and exclaimed: 'Damn you, you have done the worst against me!'

Perry calmly replied that he had merely done as he had been obliged to do. The butcher's gadfly mind once more flitted between pleasantries and curses and, unexpectedly, perhaps to make amends for his outburst, once again cajoled Perry into joining him in a drink, saying: 'Come, come, and have a glass with me, we shall be as good as friends as ever!'

Met with yet another refusal Jones reluctantly strode across the road alone in the direction of the *Westgate Hotel* pausing momentarily to beckon the constable forth with a wave of his hand. Whether it was Christmas spirit or simply a case of time on his hands, Perry at last relented and, turning on his heels, was seen to tip-toe across the muddy thoroughfare in the direction of the hotel. Now walking a mere yard or two behind Jones, it would be the most diabolical decision that PC Perry would ever make.

A nightmare would ensue. With the two men together in the hotel's cramped entrance passage Jones turned abruptly to face Perry. Without a single utterance the butcher withdrew the hideously sharp knife from his coat and plunged it into the chest of the stunned police constable. The elongated blade designed to remove meat from bone impaled the man like a fattened pig, slicing through his rib cage. With horrendous force sufficient to simultaneously cut through tunic, waist coat and two shirts Jones continued to plunge the weapon into Perry. The constable collapsed in the entrance way, frothing at the

The Westgate Hotel *seen today. Wrecked by enemy action during World War Two, it has been since rebuilt. In its original entranceway PC Perry was knifed to death.* The author

mouth, drowning in his own blood. His autopsy would later suggest that his death was mercifully near instantaneous such were the number of arteries severed and blood lost.

But what of his killer? There were at least a dozen incredulous eyewitnesses to the frenzied slaying of Perry. It was 11am and hotel patrons and staff were plentiful. Jones walked calmly through this throng with gore-spattered knife aloft and positioned himself near the bar. Pandemonium ensued. With Perry's corpse obstructing the main doorway screaming housemaids fled via a side entrance on to the busy street to raise the alarm. One brave lady, Edith Hobbs, confronted Jones and was threatened with the 'contents' of his blade for her efforts and his triumphant claim 'I have done it!'. With terrified clientele observing from a distance Jones tore open his coat and shirt and cut into his own chest several times with the lethal blade. Staggering across to a table and chair, he was bloody but conscious.

Dr Granger was called and immediately discovered there was nothing that he could do to help the stricken Perry. Turning his attention to Jones (with whom he was acquainted) the medical man was shooed away with a self pitying 'Don't waste your time on me'. Jones was wrong; his apparent suicide attempt had been somewhat non-committal. Though one of his four wounds was deep none were deemed life threatening. The first policeman on the scene, Superintendent Freeman, moved in to arrest Jones for murder. Staggering to his feet the weakened man cried out: 'Shut your mouth and let me alone; I will die as fast as I can.' Nonetheless, with his bleeding staunched Jones was dragged from the hotel and taken into custody escorted by the group of officers gathered outside.

Jones was transported to the infirmary and safely ensconced in a private ward under constant supervision of the police. At first highly loquacious in regard to the death of Perry, their prisoner would soon fall silent, his mental agitation eased with sedatives. None of the hospital staff dealing with this notorious patient made any remark as to him being under the influence of alcohol on admission. His wounds dressed and condition closely monitored, he was believed and frequently reported to be near sufficiently recovered for transfer to a prison cell.

Inquest and trial

The inquest into Perry's 'hideous assassination' would properly convene at the Town Hall on 2 January 1873 having been adjourned from the previous morning. Presided over by E B Reece, Deputy Coroner for the Cardiff Borough, there would be little in the way of legal sparring. With so many witnesses delivering powerful testimony as to Jones' culpability it would simply prove a matter of determining the state of the prisoner's sanity. Simply put, if Jones was believed sane and thus responsible for his actions he would hang. The matter of his alleged alcoholism, however debilitating to his faculties, would not be taken as mitigation. Here, the opinion of Dr Sheen supervising the prisoner's care in the infirmary would prove both decisive and damning. Assessing Jones, he said:

He appeared very feeble from loss of blood and excitement, but he was perfectly sensible, and I spoke to him. He did not appear to have been drinking. I did not see anything in the man during the time that I attended to him to indicate that he was suffering from mania or delirium. He knew full well what he was all about.

That was it. Despite a loyal yet unconvincing plea from Jones' wife as to his character, the jury quickly reached their verdict. With provocation attributed to the accused's supposed grudge against PC Perry, Jones was found guilty of wilful murder in his absence. With a death sentence taken as given the formality of sentencing would be postponed until Jones' release from hospital.

Was Jones the hardened law-hater that he was portrayed? It was alleged and widely accepted, that the motive for the slaying was a festering personal enmity towards the police constable – the murder a vicious act of retribution for an otherwise insignificant reprimand. A year earlier, Perry had needed to take Jones into custody, the incarceration however brief a source of great embarrassment to the butcher. His crime? Causing a nuisance by ringing a hand bell too loudly within the market to drum up trade. For whom the bell tolls indeed. After the murder some of Jones' acquaintances came forward to make it known that the butcher had warned some six months prior

'I have not forgotten that policeman yet. I wish I could have my revenge.' This was later allegedly corroborated by the police. Jones was perhaps even more fancifully quoted as musing 'I wonder if I shall be hung if I kill a policeman?' The veracity of this information is of course open to doubt and quite possibly an embellishment by which to thrill the local newspapers' readership. By way of contrast, according to his wife, Jones possessed nothing less than a healthy regard for the police and a general respect for the law. It's worth noting that ex-inspector Thornton had been a good friend of Jones long before his retirement from the force. So, if not a long standing grudge then why?

It is possible that the deadly assault on Perry that day was triggered by the mere spurning of Jones' invitation to accept a festive drink. One has no idea how the rejection of this perhaps drunken bonhomie played out in a tortured mind for weeks teetering on the edge of insanity. Here was a deeply paranoid man carrying a knife designed for slaughter and Perry would pay the ultimate price for non compliance. So too would Jones. His grievous self inflicted wounds delivered but moments after the slaying of Perry perhaps the strongest rebuttal of the existence of a rational and patient plan to right a perceived wrong. However improbable the jury was not to agree.

In the midst of this misery was some show of benevolence. Mindful of the impoverished state of Perry's widow and only child, members of the inquest jury had donated their fee to a benevolent fund set up on Mrs Perry's behalf. In addition to their £2 around £30 would be raised from proceeds of a benefit evening at Hutchinson & Tayleur's Circus. Also from along St Mary Street would come £26 and 17s care of Mr J W Hoffman, proprietor of the Victoria Rooms – ironically the venue in which John Jones had experienced something of a mental breakdown a few months earlier.

Infirmary

It is likely that Jones was conveyed the news of the 'guilty' verdict as gossip is hard to contain. Prostrate in a hospital bed, he was certainly fully aware of the position in the thoughts of his fellow Cardiffians and the weight of this hung heavy on his mind. Increasingly overwhelmed by his situation at night, the hospital corridors began to echo with his agonising cries of 'Murder!' Nurse Francis Mary Nathan each day at his bedside saw the health of the once recuperating man decline at an alarming rate. It was as if he no longer had the capacity to contain the thoughts of guilt within him. During the evening of Monday the 6th Jones would lie wailing pitifully while nurses desperately attempted to prevent him clawing at his wounds; a dreadful scenario that would play out over the next two days. It would prove a wretched end to a wretched life.

The funeral

On Sunday 5 January 1873, PC William Perry was buried with full honours at the old cemetery in Adamsdown. A special plot had been selected near its entrance. He was thirty-seven years old and a former military man and for whom the last eight years he had been a respected officer of the Cardiff Borough Constabulary. During this time he and his small family had resided at Montrose Cottage in Heath Street. It was reported that over 12,000 mourners and onlookers lined the route of the

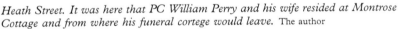

Heath Street. It was here that PC William Perry and his wife resided at Montrose Cottage and from where his funeral cortege would leave. The author

cortege such was the public outrage as to his death. Headed by the Rifle and Artillery Volunteers, twenty-five carriages snaked the route from the deceased's Riverside home into Wellington Street, over the Canton Bridge, along Duke Street, Crockherbtown and part of Roath Road. It would be a grand display of grief and municipal solidarity with the County, Borough and Docks Police Forces in attendance alongside the Cardiff Fire Brigade. The Reverend D Howell declined to deliver a funeral address at the graveside due to the 'peculiar circumstances of the occasion', wishing to 'reserve his remarks' for a later date – a coded reference to Perry's killer still being under medical supervision. The following Sunday many members of the County Borough Police force present at the graveside would attend a special service in Perry's memory at St John's Church in central Cardiff. With its theme the sins of procrastination and pride, the sermon would aptly begin:

> *Boast not thyself of tomorrow, for thou knowest not what a day may bring forth.*

John Jones' farewell would be markedly less ceremonial. He would cheat the hangman but not death itself. Although ironically reported in some newspapers as having made a full recovery, Jones would not survive beyond the middle of the week. Although in a room at the rear of the building and thus out of earshot, Perry's long funeral cortege passing the Infirmary that Sunday afternoon had driven home the enormity of his actions. Much was made of his consternation over it the following day. Doctor Sheen in attendance throughout firmly believed that his patient's mental relapse over the weekend was crucial in the loss of his ability to physically sustain himself. As his sanity waned so did his strength. He had quite simply lost the will to live. Succumbing to the infection that had set in his injuries he died at the Infirmary three days after Perry's funeral. The cause of death recorded was as a fatal haemorrhage in his lung. On 9 January 1873 his corpse was transported to the new cemetery in Cathays where, between the hours of nine and ten at night, two police constables carried out the thankless task of interring him in unconsecrated ground.

Jones would take centre stage one last time. The day of his shabby burial would see an inquest once more convened at the Town Hall; this time into the nature of his own untimely death. Again the question was to his sanity, and this having been affirmed and placed on record a week earlier, there could be only one conclusion:

We find that [John Jones] died from the effects of wounds inflicted by himself, and that he inflicted said wounds while in a sound state of mind.

The unanimous verdict was that of *felo de se* – the criminal act of 'self murder'. Some would say that he saved the executioner a job. In the eyes of the law he had been a double murderer – of both Perry and himself.

The *South Wales Daily News* of 9 January 1873 summed up the case with such clarity that it is certainly worth repeating:

Within eight days from the enactment of the tragedy the scene will therefore close, but a long time must elapse before the memory of Perry, the unfortunate victim of a man of ungovernable passion, dies out in the public mind.

Chapter 6

The Dreadful Slaying of Poor Susan Ann Gibbs Near Llanrumney Hall, St Mellons 1874

For a crime that was committed on a female fair,
In the Parish of St Mellons, As many can declare:
He murdered one he ought to cherish,
Without no cause or strife,
James Henry Gibbs without no warning
He took a precious life

Chorus

And for the deed he had to suffer,
And wish the world goodbye;
A shameful death for wilful murder
Upon the gallows high

Extracted from the ballad *Lines on the Execution and Murder of James Henry Gibbs – For the cold blooded crime he committed on the body of his Wife, Susan Gibbs,* in the early part of May 1874, near Llanrumney Hall, in the Parish of St Mellons by J W Jones.

3 June 1874. The smell! What a ghastly smell! They say that there is nothing so gut wrenching as the stench of rotting flesh. Susan Ann Gibbs' body lay flat on its back in a ditch at the foot of a hedgerow skirting Hall Farm. Not that she was recognisable to her discoverer. Hughes, a local tenant farmer, stood aghast at the state of the corpse. The recent warm weather had not

been kind to her body. Ravaged by insects and vermin, only her clothes held the flesh together. So decomposed was she that the only clear trace of violent altercation on her body was a single bruise visible on her left hand. She had met her death some three weeks prior.

On further examination of the corpse two significant facts were deduced. The first, from the semi-hidden position of the body and the ferns lodged in the hair and mouth, the victim had been attacked elsewhere and dragged to her resting place either close to death or post-mortem. The second, that cause of death was probably due to a massive haemorrhaging of blood. The victim's neck was even more sickeningly decomposed than the rest of the sorry bundle of putrid flesh and fabric – a grievous laceration to the throat resulting in a massive open wound.

Susan Ann Ingram had been born in 1831 in St Hellier on the island of Jersey to a respectable family. Securing the superior position of a lady's maid, she first travelled to England in the service of the Norton family of Sydenham. Around 1870 she moved to Lymington in the employ of a Reverend Tomlinson. A kind and responsible lady, she was well liked, particularly in respect to her care of the children. It was in this household that she was to make the fateful acquaintance of James Henry Gibbs who had been taken on as footman. Gibbs' childhood had been blighted by financial hardship and illness but with the love and encouragement of his parents he had left school a popular boy with a reputation for industriousness. Little was yet apparent as to any indication of the troubles of his later years. Promoted from running errands for local shopkeepers, he was to seek and find employment in service of a good family.

From mere friendship, Susan and James were soon to become romantically involved. It seemed that the pair shared a genuine affection for each other although Gibbs, twenty years his sweet-heart's junior, was evidently the less besotted of the two. The gap between their ages was a source of some ridicule and suspicion from some quarters but it did not impede the pair's quite serious discussion of marriage. Then in the early months of 1871 something happened to destroy their plans. For reasons unknown Susan accused Gibbs of being 'unsteady in his affections'. His furious reaction was to immediately cancel their secret wedding plans and quit his job. Leaving behind a confused and hurt Susan, he was to travel to London to seek a new position elsewhere. The heartbroken older woman verged on the edge of a breakdown as those very close to her described her love of Gibbs as tantamount to insanity. She tried in vain to trace her lover's whereabouts but letters to his father's abode were met with impatient courtesy but no disclosure of his son's address.

All this was to change by way of a truly extraordinary coincidence. Gibbs had fallen on his feet in the intervening months and secured the position of butler to the wealthy Mr Williams who owned Llanrumney Hall a few miles outside Cardiff. The Master would travel often to South Wales with his butler in tow preferring to lodge at Cardiff's *Royal Hotel* rather than his Monmouthshire home. As something of a 'below-stairs' Lothario, Gibbs became well known to the hotel's female domestic staff during their stays. The unexpected death of the hotel's proprietor, Mrs Tissot, would soon force some members of its staff to seek situations elsewhere. When one of the released hotel girls was taken on as a housemaid to the Heathfield family of Surrey it was not long before conversation with her colleagues turned to the subject of former friends and acquaintances. A casual mention of the name James Gibbs would stop the house's cook in her tracks. This kitchen employee was none other than Susan Ingram who had been in service at the Heathfield's since leaving the employ of Reverend Tomlinson. Knowing now his definite whereabouts, this was nothing less than a dream come true for the rejected Susan. Wishing to re-ignite her romance with haste she bombarded her erstwhile beau with letters to Llanrumney Hall, begging to be forgiven any wrongs of the past and hoping for a swift reunion. Susan's ecstatic missives at first met with little response but then, slowly but surely, Gibbs's letters to her began to lighten in tone. Perhaps recovering from the shock of her reappearance in his life his perfunctory replies gave way to the affection and sentiment of the early days of their original courtship. Incredibly for Gibbs he even once more broached the subject of marriage. Susan was thrilled but all was not what it seemed. Her beloved James was not quite the unattached young man that he would have her believe.

Time had not stood still for the gregarious Mr Gibbs. During his time separated from Susan a meeting would take place that would ultimately shatter the lives of all concerned. Early in January of 1872, socialising away from Llanrumney Hall, Gibbs had made the acquaintance of a local girl named Mary Jones from the nearby village of St Mellons. The pretty young chorister certainly turned the head of Gibbs and he would soon become a regular visitor at her parents' cottage. With his smile and charm he was soon seriously accepted as the young girl's suitor. If there was marriage in the air it was tragically not to be Mary walking up the aisle.

Though now otherwise amorously occupied in St Mellons, Gibbs' treacherous thoughts turned once again to the spurned Susan. She had savings and he knew it. She had been keen to accumulate enough to leave service and set up a business of her own. During the time of their initial courtship Gibbs had encouraged her in this ambition. Gibbs' cynically rekindled wooing which took place solely by exchange of letters, never once agreeing to visit her or let her travel to him. Having kept her safely at arms length, their reunion would only take place in London on route to the Southampton ship that would take them to their wedding on Jersey. With a morbid dread of the sea crossing and its allied expense Susan desperately wished to marry in England. Her mistress Mrs Heathfield had begged her to dismiss the notion of marriage to Gibbs completely. All this was to no avail. They were married on 30 July 1873 at St Saviour's Church in the town of her birth, the besotted bride footing every expense incurred. She would quickly discover that life as Mrs Gibbs would be far from sweet and her every hope and dream of a new and happy life soon cruelly dashed.

Returning to Cardiff, Gibbs wasted little time in abandoning his wife. He had already tried and failed in his ludicrous attempt to persuade her to remain in Jersey. With indecent haste he rushed back to Mary in St Mellons 'to renew his acquaintance'. During his 'unexplained' absence Gibbs had not forsaken his frequent postal correspondence with the other woman. A bemused and rejected Susan found herself newly wed and alone in a small room in *Elliot's Hotel* in St Mary Street. Gibbs had convinced her that his master would not countenance the employ of a married man and as such could never reside with him at Llanrumney Hall nor use her married name. It was a cruel deception. With only fleeting contact with her husband the written letter became his communication mode of choice. The submissive Susan dutifully obeyed. In August 1873, tiring of her accommodation, Susan sought new lodgings with a Mrs Mahoney in Dispensary Court on Working Street in the town. This kindly lady would act as both a mother and protector, offering friendship long needed by the lonely Mrs Gibbs. On his sporadic visits to his wife's new home, primarily to cadge money, the wise landlady easily saw through Gibbs and the truth of their 'secret' marriage. With no support from her husband, and now frequently short of cash, Susan was forced to find work in local hostelries. The work was rough and degrading – the type of for which she was both ill prepared and ill suited. Physically and mentally drained, Susan had only her diminishing belief in a better life in the future with her beloved James to bolster her spirits. But Gibbs' streams of written words were

Llanrumney Hall pictured today. Now a public house, it was here during the 1870s that Susan Ann Gibbs husband was employed as a footman. The author

becoming cold comfort to this isolated woman and the seeds of doubt as to his commitment to her could not be ignored.

Unsurprisingly, Gibbs remarked little to his wife of the comings and goings at Llanrumney Hall. With the master frequently away in Scotland, absorbed by his passion for hunting and shooting, the domestic duties at the large house were often few and far between. The staff would frequently find themselves idle – the devil making work for the hands of butler Gibbs in particular. From a seemingly inauspicious start Gibbs had gained a malignant reputation amongst his colleagues as being at best a boastful cad, at worst an unmitigated liar. He was distrusted and generally disliked by them all. The festering enmity between him and Miles the footman in particular would unwittingly set the slaying of poor Susan Gibbs in motion.

With village gossip rife in regard to Gibb's philandering, Miles, finding her address, took it upon himself to secretly write a letter to Susan detailing her husband's dalliance with Mary Jones. Whether to simply spite Gibbs or a genuine attempt to put right a wrong, the footman's motivation is unknown. Suffice to say this postal exposé would have potentially catastrophic ramifications for Gibbs' 'double life'. With the sordid facts of her absent partner's life laid bare an angry and humiliated Susan turned up at Llanrumney Hall to confront her husband and expose him as her legal spouse. Her visit was certainly unannounced but not unseen. Gibbs had the massive good fortune to spot his wife's approach along the driveway and frantically dashed through the house to head her off before her presence alerted his colleagues. As Gibbs hurried Susan away through a side entrance little did he realise that the scene had indeed been witnessed by some of the servants. The damage had been done. Susan needed to be both out of sight and out of mind. Sending her back to Cardiff he once again fobbed her off with the promise to write. These were to be the most twisted of love letters.

The mental abuse of the hapless Mrs Gibbs would enter a grim new phase. As if to summon up the courage and explore the possibility of being rid of the impediment that she had become Gibbs summoned his wife to a series of bizarre evening meetings in the weeks leading up to her death. Their unlikely rendezvous was the railway station at Marshfield from which they would wander aimlessly across the field and dykes into the night. What was by day picturesque by night was for the unwary treacherous – the fact of which Gibbs was only too aware. It would be easy for a person to 'accidentally' slip into a deep dyke in the pitch darkness and drown. A highly suspicious Mrs Mahoney tried in vain to dissuade her tenant from meeting up with Gibbs at such an obtuse location but, although increasingly apprehensive, the ever dutiful Susan obliged her husband. On the occasions that they met the commitment to marital together-ness that Susan so desperately craved was never voiced amid her husband's evasive small talk. Even she had a breaking point. Finally one night, spattered with mud, cold and saturated from the driving rain their 'travelling to nowhere' had become too much. A tearful and angry Susan vowed to never again meet in such a location come what may. Turning on her heels the tragic Mrs Gibbs returned forthwith to Cardiff. The apparent hesitation of the unfaithful husband had cost him dearly. Had the window of nefarious opportunity closed for James Henry Gibbs?

Once again their contact reverted to postal correspondence. Gibbs' letters to his wife, once full of forced tenderness and false promises now took on an acrimonious and vaguely threaten-ing air. He had now backed himself into a corner from which there could be but one means of escape. Susan let it be known to her friends and neighbours in Dispensary Court that she feared that her husband's newly manifested temper may lead to him hitting her. She would tragically underestimate both his increasing desperation and his ire. Openly accusing him of a continued dalliance with Mary Jones – a truth still strenuously denied, she vowed once more to return to Llanrumney Hall to confront him. With the increasing possibility of his double life being wrecked by his wife's appearance Gibbs could fob poor Susan off no longer. It was imperative that he must soon act to finally be rid of her and, to this end, he set about to cynically broker a reconciliation of sorts.

On the evening of 10 May 1874 Gibbs travelled to his wife's lodgings in Cardiff where he would spend the night with her. Mouthing untold reassurances Gibbs, with astonishing callousness, explained to his wife of his intention to finally secure lodgings for her in a cottage near the Llanrumney Hall estate. They were to live as man and wife. Susan was thrilled. This was what she had been waiting for since her wedding day. She hurried around her somewhat incredulous neighbours with her wonderful news. Gibbs would write to her to make the final arrangements. Her near childlike devotion to her husband served to nullify any lingering doubts as to his sincerity. With cruel irony the pursuit of her hopes and dreams would lure her to her death.

As instructed, at around 6.30pm on 12 May, Susan set off from Cardiff across the fields dressed in her best clothes with a raincoat and umbrella for protection from the weather. She had packed her overnight things in a small valise. Excitedly she had asked Mrs Mahoney not to wait up for her as she expected to spend the night at her new home. Gibbs had assured her that he would come to meet her along the Penylan road and from there the pair would walk on to the cottage. That evening several witnesses would see the pair separately walking towards their fatal rendezvous. Gibbs was observed to be in good spirits walking in the direction of Cardiff from Llanrumney Hall. He found time to exchange pleasantries with at least one passer by. The paths of husband and wife were ultimately to cross somewhere near the brook at Llanederyn. Matters were destined to go horribly awry. At around 8.30pm a Mr Marsden sighted the couple leaning on a gate bordering the Llanrumney Hall estate engaged in a heated argument. Gibbs was observed to be mocking his distressed wife as she was overheard to plead: 'May God rest me from my pitiful life. I am ruined!' What had transpired in the lane to shatter Susan's optimism so dramatically is not known.

It would appear that Gibbs *had* at one time given thought to lodging his wife in St Mellons as he had made tentative enquiries to this effect. Whether this was genuine or merely a ruse one will never know but it seems likely that in their conversation something had indicated to Susan that her quite lengthy travel from Cardiff that evening had once more been in vain. At around 9pm a local farmer, William Rowlands, spotted a woman fitting Susan's description briskly walking down the hill in the direction of Cardiff. This was probably the last time that she was seen alive. A short while later he would see Gibbs, who was known to him, walking along the same road to Penylan in the same direction. From evidence gleaned later it is safe to assume that after their acrimonious parting Gibbs had at first at least set out on his return journey to Llanrumney Hall only to turn tail and pursue his wife who was only a few minutes ahead. He had finally cracked. Gibbs had a task to accomplish that morality and reason could postpone no longer. His wife must be disposed of.

An exhausted Gibbs eventually arrived back at Llanrumney Hall in the early hours of the following morning. By order of the Master all doors were locked by 11pm and there was a necessity for stones thrown at the bedroom window of the room that he shared with Miles the footman to gain entrance. An agitated Gibbs did not sleep that night in his bed. In the morning light it was evident that he had spent much time frantically washing and drying his clothes. Despite their curiosity his colleagues discovered nothing of his nocturnal activities.

With great nerve Gibbs would pay a visit to his victim's lodgings only four days after her murder. His motive was two-fold: firstly to reassure Mrs Mahoney and the neighbours that his wife was 'alive' albeit incapacitated with illness and secondly rifle through her boxes of belongings. This would later prove a crucial move in his prosecution as Gibbs had on his person the only set of keys to the boxes; the very set that Susan had in her bag when she met her death. Gibbs helped himself to both her wedding certificate and her savings book explaining that his wife had urgent need of them. During a succession of audacious visits Gibbs took it upon himself to be the willing conduit for the redundant well wishes of Susan's friends. Any meeting with her was of course out of the question. At first Gibbs explained that the seriously ill Susan had travelled to Reading for a few days; later Newport. She was certainly not home to visitors. Warming to his deceitful pretence Gibbs took to writing letters to Mrs Mahoney purporting to be from his wife, reassuring her as to her improving health and promising to visit Dispensary Court in the fullness of time. Gibbs had little need to dupe Susan's family in such a manner as fortuitously for him his wife had all but been estranged from them after her controversial

The Bluebell *public house on the old Cardiff to Newport road seen today. As a centre of village life it hosted the initial inquest into Susan Ann Gibb's death.* The author

marriage to a man they intensely disliked. At his trial the reckless gambit of concocting letters (supposedly in Susan's hand) to Dispensary Court with 'the absence of any explanation as to their contents formed the most damning evidence against him'.

With the discovery and rapid identification of Susan's body, James Gibbs' arrest was a mere formality. Taken from Llanrumney Hall to Newport in the custody of Inspector Sheppard their prisoner betrayed his anxiety as he feigned incomprehension of the charge of wilful murder of his wife. Here was a man possibly undone by the vagaries of the British weather. Had the season been one of ordinary character the constant stream of water from the lands above would have washed away the effluvia that came from the body. But precisely the opposite had occurred. The unusually hot weather would hasten the decomposition of the body in situ and lead to its maybe sooner than expected discovery.

With the initial inquest held at *The Bluebell Inn* in St Mellons proceedings would soon go to the county magistrate in Newport. The resulting murder trial was to be a sensation. It was said that nothing in the county since the Chartist Riots had prompted so much interest as the discovery of Susan's body, an event the primary topic of conversation and speculation in 'every class of community' in Monmouthshire, Cardiff and beyond. With the clamour to gain entrance to the court it was noted that: 'the ladies could scarcely be aware of the horrid details that the case revealed, or it is questionable whether such extraordinary anxiety would have been manifested to hear the evidence'. A 'thin and care worn' Gibbs would meet their inquisitive gaze.

It was deduced that Gibbs had first bludgeoned his wife senseless with his walking cane. This 'weapon' was later never located. He left her prostrate; semi-conscious but alive. Gibbs knew that he had to finish the grisly deed that he started so that Susan could never again have chance to speak out. A short while later he surreptitiously returned to the nearby Hall and procured a cut throat razor or similar. Returning to his wife, Gibbs proceeded to cut her throat so deeply that her head became nearly detached from her body and dragged her 'in the last agonies of death' to the seclusion of the adjacent ditch. Taking her bag and umbrella, it was probably squeamishness not haste that prevented him from completely stripping her of clothes. It is a macabre fact worth noting that Gibbs must have later walked mere feet away from his wife's rotting corpse as he strolled along the path to and from Mary Jones' house for their frequent assignations.

Realising their virtually untenable position Mr Maddy and Mr Sawyer for the defence took the highly unusual step of calling no witnesses. With the knowledge that no one was likely to come forward with anything positive to say about their client they would rely solely on the mercy of the jury and Gibbs' own somewhat delusional self belief of innocence. It would be an all or nothing strategy. With the prosecution parading umpteen witnesses to besmirch their client Sawyer was merely to beg the jury to separate the scandalous gossip in circulation from the facts and ultimately dismiss a link between what was acknowledged as immoral behaviour and cold blooded murder. Impotently down playing the host of evidence incriminating Gibbs, Sawyer went as far as to suggest that it was likely a stranger who had killed Susan. Offering nothing to corroborate this bold statement, for Gibbs he was merely delaying the inevitable.

It should be noted that within the thankless task of mounting Gibb's defence significant questions *were* posed as to the supposed conduct of their client. Looked at impartially their doubts were not without a little justification. If it were true that James Gibbs *had* cold bloodedly murdered his wife then his actions after her death were odd indeed. Why did he kill the woman so very close to the grounds of the house in which he worked and lived? Even if the attack had no element of premeditation and the slaying the gruesome conclusion to a violent row, Gibbs made no attempt to remove the corpse from the vicinity and distance himself from the crime. It was never the case of *if* the body of Susan Ann Gibbs would be discovered but when. Why on earth didn't her killer bury her body somewhere in the acres of farmland in the vicinity? There was certainly ample time to do so. He was after all a man renowned for his guile and his economical use of the truth. By declaring to Mrs Mahoney and others that his wife had taken ill and died and that he was thus free to re-marry was tinged with madness. From the moment that the murder took place the killer had teetered on the edge of discovery. Instead of spiriting Mary Jones far away from inquisitive tongues they were to be married a mere five miles away from the scene of the crime. Did this indicate an innocent man caught up in a legal nightmare or sheer stupidity; the recklessness of a vain and arrogant womaniser driven to murder?

Mr Justice Lush presiding had little doubt. Though conceding that the evidence implicating Gibbs was almost entirely circumstantial its sheer volume was overwhelming. Such material was, in his opinion, virtually incorruptible by bias or perjury in the courtroom and as such far distanced from the foibles of man. It is doubtful that Gibbs echoed the judge's sentiment. The verdict, however anticipated by the prisoner, left him 'utterly overwhelmed and crushed in spirit'. This was the end. Gibbs having been trapped in a cycle of chronic self delusion had committed an act the aftermath of which he was ill prepared to deal with. Any attempted cover-up had been naïve in the extreme. It was agreed that, perhaps not without an element of sympathy, that with his sense of 'moral sensibility destroyed' his lies could not have failed to corrupt his mind.

Incarcerated in the prison at Usk, the chaplain's repeated pleas for Gibbs to repent were met with 'sullen and morose' indifference. The clergyman would later concede that in his opinion the prisoner was too 'hardened' to be spiritually retrievable. Such were the rumours of Gibbs' conduct in his cell that all police, warders and clergy were forbidden to converse with the press – an unprecedented move in the locality. One must spare a thought for Gibb's elderly father, tragically caught between a rock and a hard place. His own protestations to his son to acknowledge his guilt were equally rebuffed. So poor was Gibbs Snr that he was able to afford to travel to Wales just once to visit his son, his final goodbyes committed to a 'mournful, heartrending letter'. Such was the old man's poverty that a sympathetic magistrate sought to direct Gibb's £10 life assurance payout to him despite the inevitable circumstances of the prisoner's death.

With the date for execution set, the old gallows from Monmouth were removed to Usk to carry out their grim task. Their woodwork ominously painted black, a pit some 2 ft deep was dug to afford a greater drop. A deathly pall hung over the town on the eve of the hanging with ghoulish sightseers thronging the narrow streets. Many residents whose properties lay adjacent to the prison vacated their homes for the duration. This was indeed a spectacle. The execution of Gibbs was to be the first carried out in the county for fifteen years, ironically that of a man Charles Matthews convicted of slashing his wife's throat.

Having maintained his innocence and composure through-out his confinement the condemned man would now crack. Led by the governor, Colonel Millman, en route to pinioning at the gallows, Gibbs collapsed and needed to be half dragged to the platform. Finally comprehending his fate it was said that his 'yells and groans were terrible to listen to'. Repeating 'Lord have mercy on me. I die innocent!' he paused only to say goodbye to his parents. 'Sobbing and writhing in mental anguish' as he was hooded, two men were required to hold him upright until the moment of the drop. A suitably squalid end for a man whose

LINES ON
THE EXECUTION OF THE MURDERER,
JAMES HENRY GIBBS,

For the cold-blooded crime he committed upon the body of his Wife, SUSAN GIBBS, in the early part of May, 1874, near Llanrumney Hall, in the Parish of St. Mellons.

It had long been the practice to commemorate crime in song, the most celebrated form being that of a murder ballad. This is a detail of the title header of the composition related to Susan Ann Gibbs, its lyrics attributed to poet J W Jones. Author's collection

mind had first grown corrupt by the lies that he had chosen to live by and the spiral of moral bankruptcy and death as its result.

In a pitiful postscript to his execution it was accepted by some that Gibbs had after all made a confession of sorts. Whilst in Usk gaol the condemned man had sought and received visits from John Rowlands, a churchwarden and overseer of the St Mellons' parish with who he had been on friendly terms. During their final meeting Rowlands relentlessly probed Gibbs as to the knowledge of his wife's demise. After much soul searching the condemned man replied simply 'I hope she is in heaven'. This was too much for even the blindly loyal Rowlands. To the churchman the response was tantamount to an admission of guilt. He arose pronouncing: 'Gibbs you are a doomed man; it is no use deceiving you. Pray to the lord for forgiveness.' The scene in the cell was said to be so affecting that both men broke down in 'bitter tears'. Rowland's grief was such that on leaving the prison to seek solace in a local hostelry; fellow patrons witnessed him struck dumb by his inconsolable state.

'Fiancée' Mary Jones maintained a stance of both ignorance and complete innocence of any complicity in Gibbs' crime. It must be said that many doubted her word. Although she had harboured strong suspicions of his marital state it appeared on the surface that she, like poor Susan, had been seduced by the scheming Gibbs. He and Mary were to be married in June and on 28 May 1874 travelled to Cardiff in order to make arrangements with the registrar. The 'engaged' couple had been carefree enough to round off their visit to town with an afternoon at the circus. With the massive brouhaha that surrounded Gibb's committal for trial Mary left St Mellons on the advice of her parents, temporarily residing in Elm Street in the Roath area of Cardiff. She would return to her village only after the execution. She claimed that Gibbs had written her two letters whilst incarcerated but spying the tell-tale Usk postmark destroyed both unopened. With a significant number of local people, including police officers, viewing Mary's alleged naiveté less charitably the trial judge himself was prompted to put on record that he 'doubted that she merits all the censure that has been applied to her'. Perhaps he himself was unsure as to her culpability. It's worth noting his use of the word 'all' rather than the more conclusive 'any'.

One must not end this sorry tale without a final mention of poor Susan. Although not known in the village where she met her death Susan Gibbs was to be buried in the churchyard in

The rear of St Mellons Church and the final resting place of tragic Susan Ann Gibbs. Her funeral expenses were met by sympathetic local parishioners. The author

St Mellons. The vicar, Reverend J W Evans, would commence a subscription amongst the locals to raise enough money to provide a suitably inscribed headstone. A fitting act of atonement for a crime committed by one of their fellow parishioners.

Chapter 7

Henry Blatchford: Shot and Buried at Sweetman's Dairy Canton 1900

At around 3.45pm, four gun shots rang out shattering an otherwise peaceful afternoon. Although attracting some attention in the neighbourhood very few people gave considered thought that the noise might have been the calling card of a heinous crime. After all, the Fairwater Woods lay nearby – a regular haunt of sportsmen hunting pigeon. The muffled nature of the shots would suggest that they had been discharged some distance away. But had they? No tell tale smoke was seen to drift across the local gardens and the swift resumption of tranquillity would suggest that all was well. Not suspicious then surely?

At the turn of the century the Canton district of Cardiff marked the town's western fringe with an expanse of unspoilt countryside separating it from the village of Ely some two miles further west. It was still in part a semi-rural area only now beginning to succumb to the urban sprawl of the prosperous boomtown. Many Cantonians proudly regarded the suburb as a surrogate town in its own right but, more accurately, the loose congregation of roads and houses skirting the newly laid out Victoria Park at Canton's most western edge had a distinct village atmosphere. Land formally part of both the Llandaff and Ely Common, once 'as far as the tramlines go', was now beginning to be dotted with houses, the semblance of defined streets only recently taking shape. That this small community was one where everyone knew everyone else's business was a cliché clearly defined.

Everyone was familiar with Henry Blatchford if only by sight. 'A quiet, inoffensive and strictly honest man', he resided at 13 Westbury Terrace in Canton, a widower living with his daughters who kept house for him. A father of eight children, at only sixty-three years old he gave the appearance of an older man, his body stooped and complexion pallid. He had needed to seek employment even after his retirement from the nearby Ely paper mill. To this end he had regularly sold coke in the neighbourhood from a handcart and proved himself a thoroughly amenable and good-natured man – and a favourite among housewives on his round. In more recent times he had also earned money by doing odd jobs for neighbours and had struck up a particularly good relationship with a Mr Thomas Sweetman who ran a small dairy from sheds in the yard at the rear of his home in nearby Conybeare Road. He had employed Blatchford for some three months to collect and transport hay to feed his livestock. This innocuous arrangement would be the catalyst leading to the old man's horrific demise.

Perhaps familiarity does breed contempt. This is the corner of Westbury Terrace and Conybeare Road pictured today. Killer Sweetman and his victim Blatchford lived in close proximity. The author

Sometime before lunch on the afternoon of Tuesday 20 February 1900, Thomas Sweetman had entrusted Blatchford with the task of taking the cart to the King's Road Brewery, to collect feed for his cows. Having been handed 8s to pay for the grain the old man had been instructed to call into the dairy yard a short while later and collect the cart and horses once they had been made ready on their return from their milk delivery round. Blatchford carried out his instruction as he had on previous occasions. Arriving at the yard and finding that the cart had not yet been returned, he decided to occupy his time with a short visit to his sons' house in nearby Daisy Street. A few minutes later his return to the yard was witnessed by a neighbour, Mrs Hopkins. After exchanging pleasantries with her at the yard gate Blatchford entered the dairy premises away from view of the road. It would be the last time that he would be seen alive. Within a few minutes the ominous sound of gunfire would disturb the afternoon silence.

Disappearance and search

With the old man missing since Tuesday afternoon and their trawl of the area without success, Blatchford's son visited the Canton Police Station in the early hours of Wednesday morning. With a heavy heart he explained to Detective Victor Kellett his family's grave concern regarding their father's inexplicable disappearance and the fear that 'some evil had befallen him'. Kellett took the man's suspicions seriously indeed and vowed to begin his enquiries at first light, at the location of the old man's last known sighting – Sweetman's Dairy.

The crime scene and evidence

Detective Kellett, accompanied by a neighbour William Smith, quietly entered the small yard and observed the young Tommy Sweetman, the dairy man's son, hunched over a small fire. The youth, startled by the pair, lurched backwards and was apprehended by the police officer. A substantial piece of un-burnt cloth – apparently a section of a velvet-collared garment – was rapidly dragged from the flames. 'These belong to the old man. That is Blatchford's overcoat. I know it!' exclaimed Smith. He was sadly correct.

A patch of freshly-raked earth and manure was the telltale sign of Blatchford's unholy resting place. His partially-clothed body lay just six inches beneath the surface. Hurriedly, Detective Kellett went at the ground with a shovel to expose its grisly contents. His urgency with the tool would get the better of him – an incautious thrust succeeded in near scalping the corpse of the unfortunate Blatchford as it lay in the earth. Quickly, the dead man's face was revealed 'ghastly and bloody, besmeared beyond recognition'. Finally disinterred, the victim was found to have a severe shotgun wound to the right side of his chest. The resulting shattering of part of his rib cage had caused grievous penetration of the liver, heart and lungs. The firearm had been discharged no more than a few feet away. The wounding was such that death was likely to have been instantaneous, the post-mortem later carried out by police Surgeon Dr Wallace deducing that he had died not twenty-four hours earlier.

At sixteen years of age the young Thomas Henry Sweetman (known as 'Tommy' to differentiate him from his father) had lived a short and blighted life. Suffering both physical and mental infirmity he had endured severe fits as a baby. His often erratic behaviour lead to 'queer things', though never with

An artist's impression of Sweetman senior's dairy yard, the scene of the killing and impromptu burial of William Henry Blatchford. Author's collection

SCENE OF THE TRAGEDY.
The cross on the left indicates the grave where the body was found.

violence but it eventually resulted in a year's detention in Bridgend Asylum for the Insane. Returning home after his release he had busied himself in helping with small tasks at his parents' dairy and was a reserved yet popular young man with his Canton neighbours. What on God's earth had led him to the position here in the yard that afternoon was not known to anyone other than himself.

There was sufficient physical evidence at the scene to damn the hapless Sweetman Jnr and any accomplice. Strong daylight exposed blood spatters across a section of the milking shed's interior while a flask containing shot remarkably similar to that lodged in the corpse was found on a shelf at the rear. Indeed, marks on the barrel of the shotgun found in the hayloft of the adjacent shed indicated that it had been recently fired. This is to say nothing of the burning of items of the deceased's apparel.

Admission of guilt?

Tommy Sweetman was arrested and immediately taken into custody, protesting his innocence all the while. He initially swore that he had absolutely no knowledge of the circumstances surrounding the old man's murder. But, during the afternoon, as news of further evidence incriminating him filtered through, he changed tact and called on a detective to listen to his 'admission'. He explained: 'I had better speak the truth. It will be better for me. I went out with father and mother with the cart to sell milk and got out of the cart at Penhill and saw Thompson. Then we went to his house. We then went to the cowsheds in our yard. I fetched the gun and Thompson shot the old man.'

John Thompson aka Jack Sullivan, aged forty, the pathetic companion and fellow defendant of Thomas Sweetman. The two had first met while incarcerated in the Bridgend Asylum. Author's collection

Before the police could act upon this information a dramatic twist to the case would unfold. At around 6pm on the evening of 21 February, forty-year-old John Thompson (aka Sullivan) presented himself at Canton Police Station in connection with the crime. This had been a pre-emptive move as local gossip had reached his Daisy Street home suggesting that he had been implicated in Blatchford's death. He, like Sweetman, had recently been incarcerated in the Bridgend Asylum. They were indeed acquainted – much to Sweetman's father's chagrin. It was true that they enjoyed a friendship of sorts and were often seen in each other's company.

That evening young Sweetman was formally charged with murder along with his alleged accomplice, Thompson. Standing before William James, Chief Inspector of Police, the two prisoners made an odd and pitiful pair – the verbose Sweetman along side the taciturn Thompson who held both his temper and his silence in the face of the younger man's accusations. Now, with the discovery of specks of blood on Sweetman's sleeve itself, he found need to expand upon his story. Persisting with the assertion that he had no part in the killing, Sweetman now claimed to have been coerced by Thompson into removing the body from the shed and into the yard for burial, thus coming into contact with Blatchford's blood. This was too much for even the stoic Thompson. 'F—ing perjurer!' he exclaimed and a scuffle ensued, the two men having to be separated by police.

The trial

The magisterial inquiry would commence on Thursday 22 February 1900 at Cardiff Town Hall. It would be presided over by Mr E Bernard Reece, the Borough

The accused, Thomas Sweetman. Bluntly described as a 'stunted and deformed youth', he would try to make amends for his physical appearance by donning smart clothes and a striking black and white checked scarf while in the witness box.
Author's collection

Coroner. From the outset it was stated that if necessary a plea of insanity would be set up on behalf of both prisoners. The trial would be long-winded and laborious with copious witness statements and frequent adjournments halting its progress.

For a mentally troubled man in the care of his mother, Thompson would give a creditable if understandably nervous performance in the witness box. He articulately highlighted the fact that there was not one witness who could place him in Tommy Sweetman's company on the afternoon in question and, furthermore, that he had proof that he was a mile away in town at the time of the killing. In stark contrast, Sweetman 'stared about the court and acted more like a messenger waiting for an answer than anything else'. One cannot be sure if this constituted an act of defiance on his part or whether he truly had not the capacity to comprehend the proceedings. Either way, Sweetman's version of events would be soon decimated by the weight of evidence against him.

Sweetman could proffer no explanation as to why property belonging to the victim was found in his possession. The old man's knife, matches, pipe and tobacco pouch had been secreted in Sweetman's coat pocket. Of the 8 shillings known to have been given Blatchford only 6 were found. It was reckoned that the missing cash had been used by the youth to purchase the container of paraffin that he had used to fuel the fire by which he attempted the burning of Blatchford's overcoat. With the killer's fragile state of mind one can only speculate as to his reasoning for attempting to destroy just this one item of clothing. The victim could easily have been identified by his other garments.

One by one, witnesses who had observed and encountered young Sweetman the afternoon of Blatchford's disappearance were called to give testimony. The cumulative effect of their observations would prove decisive. Annie Thompson, a neighbour of the Sweetmans whose property overlooked their yard, recalled looking out of her window after hearing the gun shots and seeing the accused standing motionless with head bent out side the shed in which the murder was said to have taken place. Jane Hopkins of Ivy Street, who had watched Blatchford enter but not leave the dairy that day, told of her daughter visiting the premises some thirty minutes after the sound of the shots. Her request to buy some milk was swiftly and inexplicably refused by a visibly shaken Sweetman. More damaging still was the statement by two young boys, Harry Hansford and John Thomas. Whilst playing football on common land bordering the rear of the dairy yard, Hansford observed the accused nailing shut a 'trap door' which when open allowed a view inside the shed from the common. Venturing closer, his playmate Thomas, swore that he heard a groan emanating from inside the shed. Sweetman wasted no time in ordering him away telling them that the sound from inside was that of a sick cow. If their recollection was accurate then an even more grisly aspect to the killing would emerge. The boys were convinced that they heard the third shot *only after* Sweetman's return to the shed after shooing them away. Was it the case that the old man lay dying all the while awaiting the final shots that would release him from his agony?

By the early evening of the murder it would seem that young Sweetman's guilt had begun to engulf his troubled mind. Another milkman, John Corcoran, would call at the Sweetman dairy. In the witness box he told of Tommy Sweetman feverishly quizzing him as to having seen his father. When he replied to the contrary Tommy Sweetman begged him to forget having ever having seen or spoken to him here on the pretext that his father would be angry that he was at home neglecting his chores. He was also eager to know if Corcoran had any business in the yard the following morning. Their strained meeting was to conclude with a clumsy attempt to buy his silence with a sixpence, Tommy cajoling Corcoran: 'Here's the price of a drink Jack. Drink my health.' Corcoran was naturally perplexed and had angrily refused to accept the bribe and left the premises. It seemed that Tommy had, that afternoon, shockingly entered an adult world of crime and deceit with which his childlike mind found it near impossible to cope.

Motive
With the subdued testimony of his parents, young Tommy's movements that ruinous afternoon would become apparent.

Thomas Sweetman, accompanied by his wife and son, left their dairy by cart to commence their round at around 2 o'clock. Nearing Romilly Crescent Sweetman Snr alighted the cart with the usual arrangement that it would pick him up on its return route from Llandaff. His wife explained that Tommy, in her husband's absence, a few minutes later jumped off the cart and without explanation walked off in the direction of Cathedral Road. Having been missing for approximately two hours young Sweetman reappeared on Wyndham Crescent rejoining his parents on the cart for the short journey home. His parents had been completely unaware of how their son had occupied his time whilst away from them.

Sweetman's father, clearly harassed by the inquest's proceedings, doggedly spoke up for his son. He affirmed that young Tommy had indeed been on good terms with the deceased; the lad had even shown the old man how to handle the horse and cart. With this small detail, nothing more than a footnote in his heart-rending testimony, the dairyman would shed light on the whole sorry situation. It transpired that Sweetman Snr had, two months prior, dismissed his son from the job of fetching the cows' grain, having, for unspecified reasons, been 'dissatisfied' with his efforts. It had been the lad's primary duty since his release from the asylum and his return to Canton. Sweetman Snr had immediately entrusted Henry Blatchford with the task – the execution of which had led the old man to the dairy that day and thus to his death.

Here was the key to crime. The killing *had* seemed without motive. Detectives knew that with Blatchford being of such limited means and only ever carrying a small amount of money that the notion of robbery had to be discounted. The slaying was likely an act of extreme recklessness prompted by a childish jealousy. The resentment of the old man taking over the duties that were once his, however trivial to the sane, was likely enough to push a tortured mind to countenance murder. Moreover, an element of possible premeditation was apparent. Had the leaving of his parents and the cart and his returning to the yard early been part of his plan to confront Blatchford alone? He was certainly aware that the old man would be waiting there for the cart and horses' return.

The verdict

Only on retirement of the jury did Sweetman Jnr appear to finally comprehend the severity of the crime. Having long affected a slightly detached, uninterested air during the proceedings he at that moment began to violently sob with his head pressed tightly in his hands. Perhaps, even in his semi-childlike state he knew that time would soon be called on his violent and needless caper. Summing up the coroner observed: 'It was a terribly cold blooded murder, and the only thing that they could hope was that Sweetman was so far out of his mind that he was not responsible for his action.'

The jury were reminded that the only accusations against Thompson were made by Sweetman himself – nothing corroborated by any witness. The implication was clearly that the word of a 'madman' was of little value at all. This would have been a sad indictment of the legal system had Sweetman's allegations against his cohort not been blatant lies. Detective Kellett concluded that in his opinion it would have been 'impossible for Thompson to be anywhere near the murder, and that in fact he had no hand in it.'

After a ten minute deliberation the jury would return a verdict of wilful murder on Sweetman with no mention of Thompson at all. Thompson's solicitor, Mr Phillips, immediately called for his release. The coroner's response betrayed uncertainty: 'As far as I'm concerned he is free but the police have to bring him up before the magistrates. I don't know if they will discharge him.' Thompson was indeed kept in custody before being released on bail the following week. With all charges dropped the innocent man would return home to the care of his mother and live out his days in obscurity.

Young Tommy Sweetman would not be so lucky. With his case transferred to the Glamorgan Assizes he would not wait long to learn his fate. The trial was brief and its culmination probably a foregone conclusion. Sweetman cut a pathetic figure in the dock. Medical officers acting for both the prisoner and the prosecution were unanimous in their view that Sweetman was unfit to plead due to his mental deficiency. With the jury dismissed, the presiding judge, Mr Justice Bucknill, ordered

Sweetman to be taken way for incarceration in a criminal lunatic asylum to be detained at Her Majesty's pleasure.

Cardiff Board of Guardians

On news of the guilty verdict, the Cardiff Board of Guardians whose stated remit 'was to see to the removal of people of unsound mind' wasted little time in washing their hands of any moral responsibility for Tommy Sweetman after his return to his family a year earlier – and thus his subsequently murderous actions. The Board's Warrant Officer, a Mr Pritchard, pointedly informed the press that he believed the accused to be mentally ill still and was the sole responsibility of his father into whose care the Board had reluctantly released the youth. Referring to their acquiescence to Sweetman Snr's impassioned plea for the return of his son, F J Beavan of the Board declared unequivocally: 'This is a lesson to the Board that it ought never to be influenced by outside considerations such as were brought before us in this case. I hope the Board will not move too readily in these cases in the future.'

Whilst publicly voicing these disclaimers, even the venerable members of the Board would admit that their former charge had not once shown an inclination to violence whilst in their care.

A tragedy

Perhaps the real tragedy is of Thomas Sweetman and his wife Mary Jane. The loving father had worked relentlessly to persuade the authorities to release his only son back into his care and return to the family home. He had suffered the dual disappointment of his son's admission to an approved school refused – due to his mental condition – and later the Board of Guardian's declination to allow him to travel to Ireland to live with an uncle. The murder weapon was a gun that Sweetman Snr himself had borrowed from a friend to go rabbit shooting in Peterstone. He would ruefully declare that to the best of his knowledge his son had never before even handled a gun let alone fired one. Their life would now be in ruins. They had to now live with the knowledge they may have been woefully misguided all along. Perhaps their son *was* unfit for a '*life*' outside the institution – truly a danger both to himself and others. Had they, in securing their son's release, in reality done him the utmost damage and precipitated the death of a defenceless old man?

The funeral and conclusion
This had truly been a 'local' crime, deeply affecting those who had been acquainted with both Blatchford and the pitiful Sweetman Jnr. It would appear to have counted for little in the hustle and bustle of the wider environs, perhaps prompting vague interest at best. The Edwardian era's rapid house build-ing programme would come to close the gaps between the surrogate villages and hamlets bordering the town embracing them as fully fledged suburbs as Cardiff approached city status in 1905. It would herald the ending of an era in which the sometimes insular focus of the town's outlying reaches would be directed to its commercial centre; urbanization blurring the boundaries between urban and rural – the 'inner city' expanding into the once leafy lanes and their cottage dwellings. Henry Blatchford's funeral would stand testament to this outmoded parochialism. On 26 February 1900, the victim's remains were transported from his home and along Conybeare Road 'thronged with people anxious to have a last look at proceedings . . . the cortege being a lengthy and imposing one.' In death as in life the deceased had been a local celebrity 'respected . . . by neighbours and others residing in the Western end of Canton.' The assembled masses preceding the funeral cortege would ensure its slow progress up to the junction of King's Road and Cowbridge Road. Then, as it progressed towards Canton Bridge, the crowds began to noticeably thin, mourners and onlookers drifting away, their job done. Once away from Canton and over the river into the town 'proper' the absence of mourners was evident and the funeral procession would go forth to the new cemetery in Cathays with 'no particular curiosity shown by the public'.

Chapter 8

The Unsolved Murder of Harriet Stacey (aka Harriet England/Kate England) Grangetown 1904

St Valentine's Day 1904. A time for lovers, a time for secrets a time for romance? Not here – dark secrets only. Breathless whispers and pledges in a private world closely guarded. It could be said that Harriet Stacey had too many friends. Should we be indiscrete and whisper too many lovers? Her home at 41 Saltmead Road in the working class district of Grangetown, west of the River Taff's divisive route through Cardiff town would make a curious love nest. An area short on wealth but kempt and respectable – morally if not geographically much removed from its notorious near neighbour Tiger Bay.

Poor Mrs Stacey lay dead on her bed. The scene in her room was a 'Grand Guinol' tableau as gruesome as any viewed by those possessed of both the penny admission and a morbid curiosity in Madame D'Arcs Wax Works display in town. No gas lamps flicker here – the pitch blackness only illuminated by a quick burning match held in a trembling hand. And what a sight it was. Half-turned to the side in an approximation of a foetal position, her modesty was spared by a nightdress scarcely ridden up and the partial covering of the bedclothes. Her hands clasped as in prayer contrasted with her contorted facial features – her tongue swollen and black lolling obscenely from her mouth. A rope was tied around her neck as a noose. Mystifyingly, as is so much connected with this case, the rope is long enough to be slackly threaded up around the middle of the head bedstead and trail back down the length of the bed to be wound loosely around its foot but not tied. There is contradiction even here.

The house in which Harriet Stacey mysteriously met her death, pictured in 1904. This section of Saltmead Road would be later named Stafford Road, the then distinct Saltmead neighbourhood long consumed by the greater Grangetown area. Author's collection

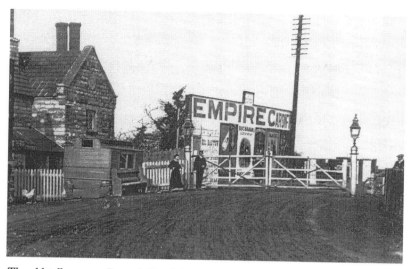

The old toll-gate on Penarth Road in Grangetown. Cardiff Public Libraries Collection

Harriet Stacey's neighbour – Mrs Williams – was to identify the rope as that used by the deceased as a washing line, other contemporary reports have it as a linen bed sheet. One and the same?

Although recognised as 'a very reserved person' and dignified in the baring of her physical illness, neighbours of the victim duly noted the 'many and frequent' visitors to her home. These in the main were said to be gentlemen of the 'seafaring class' – Victorian journalistic code for those seeking prostitutes. One of her physical afflictions would draw direct attention to the numerous comings and goings at the Saltmead Road house. Close associates of the deceased could arrive and gain entrance unannounced. They were instructed to put their hand through the letterbox where a tug on a piece of string would turn the lock and thus open the door. For those not in this select group of associates privy to the routine with the latch key a vigorous banging of the door knocker was necessary to bring the visitor to the attention of the partially deaf Mrs Stacey – and, in so doing, all and sundry in the quiet street too.

It is inadequate to say that she had lead a double life for she was adept at assuming and making work more identities than that. Forty-nine at her death, she had married young to John

Stacey, a railway engineer and respected member of the community in their native city of Hereford. In a foretaste of later indiscretions she was forced to separate from her husband after a clumsy affair with a lodger had been exposed. Leaving her family and friends behind her she relocated to Cardiff in 1901. By this time the unfortunate Mrs Stacey had been diagnosed as both physically ill and mentally unstable – conditions that she must have struggled to hold at bay. During her short life in Cardiff her skill at being economical with the truth succeeded in creating a wilful confusion of personas still not unravelled even after her death. Early newspaper accounts of her grisly demise erroneously portrayed her as a forty-five-year-old from Nottingham, her parents of 'high respectability'. To her neighbours she became Mrs Harriet England – some-times 'Kate England'. She shared her Saltmead Road house with her 'husband' – Mr England, a 'Dutch Marine Engineer' whom was often at sea. Luckily for him the timing of one such voyage would be a water tight alibi for involvement in her death. The third part of this furtive ménage a trois came in the shape of Mr William Henry Warren, an unemployed dock labourer, who posed (and was accepted by her neighbours) as her 'brother'. After her death it became evident that Mr

England and Mr Warren were acquainted and on friendly terms so one can only speculate as to their knowledge of their respective relationships with the erstwhile 'Mrs England'. To her children, Harriet Stacey, portrayed herself as the *housekeeper* in residence for the mysterious Mr England and, not wishing to upset this apple-cart, deterred any visits by her offspring with the curious yet

The enigmatic Harriet Stacey. An outwardly respectable middle-aged woman, she was to take on several identities, becoming something of all things to all people person. Author's collection

highly convenient excuse that Mr England, 'as a foreigner, was averse to her having visitors'.

In the twilight gloom of that fateful February evening, agitated by the fact that his close friend Mrs Stacey had relayed no prior warning of her forthcoming 'absence', William Henry Warren had only managed to gain entry to her home at the third attempt. Failing to turn the latch as usual he contrived to file down his own front door key to turn the lock. Constable Francis Scowcroft, alerted whilst walking his beat on nearby Tudor Street, was the first policeman at the scene. He wasn't alone for long as the local constabulary took his findings very seriously. At first the investigation was headed up by Inspectors Yelland and Butler from the local Grangetown Police Station. With an admission of growing uncertainty considerable extra manpower was drafted in under the supervision of two senior detectives from the Central Police station and the summoning of Marmaduke Pittard, divisional police surgeon.

Having the misfortune of being the individual who discovered the corpse, Warren was detained and questioned half-heartedly for only a few hours. Eloquently protesting his innocence, he was described as being 'gentle as a lamb' by Harriet Stacey's neighbour who believed him to be her brother. Displaying shock and tenderness towards the dead woman, he emphatically refused to criticise the police for his brief incarceration. On his release and elimination as a suspect the investigating officers were left grasping at straws. Of the only other two named associates of the deceased (both her 'Hereford' and 'Cardiff' husbands) neither could ever have been realistically considered as the culprit. Intriguingly, while still a suspect (however short-lived) it is suggested that Warren was asked by

John Stacey, the victim's husband. He appeared to be unaware of the domestic complications in the life of his spouse. Author's collection

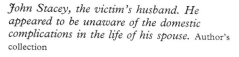

an associate if he suspected that a *certain person* was the killer of Harriet Stacey. He hesitantly responded 'I should like to know where that person is'. Whomever he was referring to we shall never know as this matter was never broached at the inquest. It leaves hanging in the air yet another tantalising thread whose potential value to the enquiry will be forever unknown.

That she was in the habit of taking week long sojourns by train to London is related by both Mr and Mrs Williams and Warren. The only verifiable fact here however is that she frequently spent weeks away from her home – nothing to establish her destination other than what she herself told people. These short 'holidays' could be of scant significance in the scheme of things but there was little in the way of family or friends to connect her with London or prompt her visits. Could her assignations have taken place slightly closer to home? During the week she lay dead a telegram had arrived at her house. Sent from Gloucester, it simply queried her 'long silence'. Read out at the inquest, its sender would remain a mystery – unknown to any in attendance. Was its message genuine or a clever way of staging a lack of recent contact between a killer and his victim? Perhaps a missing part of this macabre jigsaw or simply another 'friend' in need.

Mrs Stacey had been intending to soon vacate her house and leave Cardiff for good. She had confided as much to her neighbour Mrs Williams and purchased a trunk from her in which to transport her belongings. Her reasons for planning to move away from Cardiff are open to speculation. After her death those close to her either did not know or chose to hold their silence. It may of course been a purely innocent desire to explore pastures new but in this milieu where guile and subterfuge are endemic there is very little in the way of purity or innocence. Remember that Harriet Stacey's other life (lives?) was looming perilously close. With one daughter treading the boards in the nearby town of Newport and now, God forbid, another recently relocated to the very nearby district of Canton, her past had been delivered to her doorstep. The fear of un-announced visits from her daughters must have been acute and the potential for a bedroom farce of dual identities and play acting too agonizing to contemplate. The pretence of propriety is only easily maintained through postal correspondence and strictly regulated house calls. It's equally plausible that she was wishing to extricate herself from one of her relationships – one of the men in her life becoming too demanding, too intimidating. Perhaps it was he who was to call time on their friendship in such a gruesome way.

From the outset detectives were convinced that her death was a grisly adjunct to robbery. Her killer was too a thief and had made off with whatever cash she had secreted at home. This assumption of theft as a motive for murder is tentative in the extreme and probably only succeeded in leading the police up an investigative blind alley. If she did have a 'getaway fund', exactly how much money *had* she accumulated – and by what means? If one accepts her Post Office paying-in book as correct it accounts for £41 0s 5d. A tidy sum then. There is no way of knowing how much (if any) she had stashed at home. Surely only her inner most circle of friends could have had any real idea. Her neighbours in the wider vicinity regarded her as 'possessed of means' – independently so according to her close friend Warren. Even a newspaper report thought that it was worth noting that her furniture 'is superior to that usually found in houses of the same kind'. One neighbour's comment that she was 'not short of a few quid' is more based on gossip than evidence but it seems that she *was* financially comfortable – albeit by quite modest standards. At the inquest her *real* husband stated quite categorically that he had made her no 'pecuniary allowance' during their years apart. This was in complete contradiction to the widely held view of her kith and kin that her Mr Stacey had 'made provision that she should never come to want' even though she had 'forfeited all monetary support'. Perhaps for the reputedly kind-hearted Mr Stacey to admit such generosity in public was a step too far.

Under any circumstances, one of the most bizarre aspects in this baffling case was the discovery of a journal written by the deceased. Luridly referred to in the press and later at the inquest, its specific content was never quoted, deemed far too shocking and corrupting for the general public by the patrician authorities. One can only deduce that it shed no light on the identity of her killer. What manner of depravity fuelled her writings one will never know – the diary has long since been lost. A contemporary newspaper report claims that she had:

> ... *passed through the crisis incidental to womanhood, and the best medical advice in Hereford pronounced that she must either die or suffer such mental derangement as would leave her periodically with little control over her actions. Whether this illness was to cause the moral looseness of Mrs Stacey can only be decided by experts in lunacy, but that she suffered acutely from time to time after her departure from Hereford is conclusively evidenced by a series of remarkable, if not absolutely unique, entries in her diary which was found in her house, and in which there had been recorded quite recent events which, without this explanation, would strike its readers as showing a depravity of mind of the worst type.*

Another report of the diary divulges its role as a bookkeeping tool as well as a hint to its other more salacious content:

> *The unfortunate woman appears to have possessed remarkable business and methodical habits for one of her class. She kept a diary in which she made all sorts of peculiar entries including money received and paid away, so that at the end of each week she knew exactly what her financial position was. The entries in the diary are of a remarkable nature, and are of such a character that they cannot be disclosed.*

Fascinating that even at the inquest the substance of the diary was deemed so disturbing that it had to be suppressed. The vital point here is the use of the word 'business' and the record of 'money received'. Bare in mind that her role of 'housekeeper' to the mysterious Mr England was most likely in name only and, that she received an allowance from her estranged husband in Hereford, vehemently denied by him. How then *did* she support herself financially? The juxtaposition of written entries both 'financial' and 'depraved' leads the reader to the logical conclusion that payment was being received for some form of sexual service the detail of which rests within the parameters of our imagination. But is this necessarily the truth? Is it possible that, despite investigators' heavy-handed hints to the contrary, the deceased's enthusiastic sexual appetites were not enacted for financial gain? This would be a scandalous – possibly incomprehensible – proposition for the good citizens of turn of the century Cardiff. Was her illness, obliquely alluded to in the press, a form of nymphomania apparently caused or exacerbated by her menopausal condition? A jarring thought even today. Her sin a desperate craving for intimacy and sexual intercourse purely for enjoyment's sake? As one columnist portentously concluded, her life would one day provide:

> *. . . matter for earnest thought for students of the effect of the potent influences of mental and physical pain upon morality.*

Although the positioning of her body and the convoluted tying and looping of the rope was clear evidence at the scene negating the possibility of Mrs Stacey having taken her own life, the local rumour mill was rife with talk of 'suicide' from the outset. Gossip and conjecture would intensify to fill the vacuum created by the police's utter bewilderment and lack of suspects or motive. It was speculated that her death scene was a faux 'hanging' invented by her killer but left unfinished – hastily abandoned for reasons unknown. Might that explain the use of the excessively long rope twisted around her bed? With knowledge of her mental anguish and the post-mortem discovery of a large internal cyst that must have been at times excruciating, a family member would later admit that:

> *At any time I would have not been surprised to hear that she had destroyed her life, for she was a woman who made little demonstration of her trials and ill health, and I know what the doctors had said some years ago.*

Death was determined to be strangulation, from behind, executed by powerful hands. With Coroner E B Reece being adamant that the deceased in no way could have strangled herself and the jury at the inquest returning a verdict of 'Wilful murder by some person or persons unknown' one would have thought that the notion of suicide would have been laid to rest. Not so. The 'myth' would persist even into the 1950s with a short newspaper article recounting the case. It's title *Suicide? Or was Harriet Strangled?* would tantalise the reader but offered no evidence to support anything other than murder. Brief mention of the inquest's coroner, E B Reece later doubting his original conclusions appears groundless and somewhat fanciful. In the absence of the definitive, a concrete motive, a named killer; 'truths' – no matter how implausible will always expand to fill the void.

Helping the killer

It's conceivable that, wholly oblivious to their luck, the fastidious routines of his victim would deal the killer a most fortuitous hand. Harriet Stacey was last seen alive on the afternoon of Sunday 7 January by her neighbour Mr Williams. With her customary Monday laundry not commenced the next morning it is safe to say that, alongside evidence of the body's decomposition and unread newspapers littering her hallway, she had lain dead a whole week before discovery. Unmissed by her friends and neighbours attributing her absence due to an impromptu trip to London, the killer's trail could grow very cold indeed. Her window blinds were invariably drawn to shield her unusual domestic life from prying eyes so little was thought of the house remaining in darkness for the week. Entry to the property would have been silent. It was deduced that the killer was acquainted with the latch key routine and entered the property via the front – the back having been bolted from the inside. He had even dead-locked the door and removed the key as he exited thus preventing any other regular callers' entry to the property in their accustomed fashion. Next door neighbour Williams had sworn that he had heard noises coming from the house after dark during the week. This would suggest that the killer had made return visits to the property after her death. If the theft of her savings was the motive of the crime then surely, her storage trunk prized open, all money would have been taken at the time of her killing. It would have been reckless in the extreme to return to the scene – and for what?

Other motives

To understand the crime perhaps, unlike the constabulary, we should turn the notion of 'robbery' on its head. Could the systematic 'ransacking' of each room in the house in reality have been the killer's frantic removal of any trace of his *own* connection to the victim by way of correspondence or personal effects? Although wardrobes and cupboards had been haphazardly pulled open, their contents strewn, *nothing* belonging to the victim could be identified as actually being missing from the property. Remember that no one knew how much (if any) money was in the house other than Harriet Stacey herself. Her jewellery remained untouched. The remains of recently burned paper in the hearth were inexplicable at the time. Could the 'chopping' noise heard by Williams during the week be the fashioning of sticks for the fire? In this twilight world of unspoken sexual desire with Harriet Stacey at its centre how long could jealously be kept at bay? She was known to be a 'shared' woman. Had she become far too embroiled with one man to the murderous displeasure of another? It is even feasible that she was caught 'in flagrante' by one of her many suitors. There was clear evidence that she had not been alone in her bed prior to her death but there was no way to ascertain exactly *how* long before. Could the killer have been her erstwhile bed-mate? Is it plausible that her death was the result of an accident and not murder at all? Could it have been the result of a morbid sex game that had simply gone too far? Without Harriet Stacey's scandalous diary one has no way of knowing if she and her partners were conversant with the fetish of erotic asphyxiation believed to heighten the sexual act. Did her lover flee the scene in blind panic only to return at a later date to remove his belongings? As always, her unseemly demise begs more questions than answers. As one commentator so aptly recorded:

> *The more the crime is investigated the more mysterious and inexplicable it appears.*

Harriet Stacey was buried at the new Cardiff cemetery in Cathays. Like at all good funerals the skies darkened and the heavens opened on all and sundry. Strikingly, it is said, the vast majority of mourners were women. How ironic then at the funeral of a woman whose life (and death) had been so inextricably shaped by her dealings with men. Her murderer has never been identified.

Postscript

Just the day after Harriet Stacey's body was discovered, a short walk away at Cardiff's recently-built Grand Theatre, a new play had opened to much acclaim. Directed by the lauded Victor du Cane, the four-act drama was entitled *Sins of the City*. A deliciously grim irony that well illustrates the well worn cliché of 'art imitating life'.

Chapter 9

Hilda Medd (aka Hilda Mead): Death following an Illegal Abortion
Ely
1927

In recent years the far western Cardiff suburb of Ely has suffered from the social unrest of the age and for a time in the early 1990s became a byword for disturbance and disorder in the national press. Its fiercely proud local residents have now done much to repair this damage. It was not always like this. The large estate had originally been conceived in the mid 1920s as a 'Garden Suburb' housing project set by the council to alleviate serious overcrowding and deprivation in its inner city areas. Cardiff already boasted the much smaller Rhiwbina Garden Village on its rural fringe. These were the 'homes fit for heroes' of Lloyd George's post-Great War promise. The clamour to reside in these spacious semi-detached dwellings and bungalows amidst lawns and trees was huge. With its wide roads and well constructed housing stock this was an ambitious scheme and not for nothing was the area's main thoroughfare dubbed 'Grand Avenue'.

The housing project was not without its detractors. A City Council meeting in the January of 1927 thrashed out proposals for a number of smaller maisonettes to be built among the larger homes. Alderman Howell JP, as Chair, was less than impressed with the call to provide associated green spaces. These *after all* would be occupied by working-class tenants. Rather condescendingly he pronounced that 'gardens though desirable of course,

Stanway Road in Ely seen today. During the 1920s this was the recently built home of the unfortunate Hilda Medd. The author

were wasted on many people'. They were to be grimly ironic words. Some residents like Mrs Hilda Medd of Stanway Road found the use of a garden vital; a plot of one's own. No seeds to be sewn here to bring forth new life rather a patch to bury the little dirty secrets of the dead.

Mrs Medd

January 1927. Mrs Medd was once again pregnant and, rather awkwardly for her, her marine engineer husband – now long at sea – was not the father. Her belly now swollen to the extent that her condition would soon become apparent to all she resolved to do what she had twice done before. Her ten-year-old daughter Irene was instructed to take a message to an old friend and neighbour from their days in Grangetown's Paget Street.

Around lunchtime on Sunday 2 January the man, Reginald Oliver Morris, duly arrived at Medd's house at 69 Stanway Road. They had last met in November of the previous year for reasons never disclosed. Morris was a quack physician of the lowest order; a masseur ready and willing to rub linament into the muscles of the afflicted. As far as her children and neighbours were concerned Morris had been summoned to alleviate the rheumatic pain in her collar bone. The truth was rather less wholesome. Morris was familiar to a cabal of local women as an amateur abortionist; someone who one could turn to in times of need. A man for hire, he was ever willing to travel and perform his grim service for a price.

In her bedroom away from prying eyes Morris tended to Medd's body and plied her with pills, returning the next morning to administer more of the same. A frankly incredible and grotesque pantomime would play out over the following seven days on the Ely estate.

During the morning of Monday 3 January two friends of Medd, a Mrs Roberts and Mrs Davies visit her in Stanway Road. Their arrival is in no way coincidental. Both guests are pregnant and Morris undertakes to 'massage' the pair. That night, stupefied by pills purchased by Morris from Huxley's Bridge Street chemist, Mrs Roberts painfully miscarries at the home. Morris will play the role of both terminator and undertaker. The Tuesday sees Roberts carry her dead baby boy back to Medd's house where Morris relieves her of the lifeless body and disposes of it on the fire burning in the sitting room hearth. A job well done 'Dr' Morris but what of the lady of the house?

For the last three days she too has been subject to internal manipulation and fed a diet of pills and alcohol. Her body's rejection of the baby is taking far too long and the experienced Morris knows it. For Medd, Monday's discomfort has become Tuesday's agony. Finally, on the Wednesday in a great mass of blood and screaming, Hilda Medd loses her child. With no coal left for the fire Morris realises that he must find another way of being rid of this little baby girl and sets about doing so in the garden. But something is wrong and Hilda Medd is not recovering from her ordeal. She has become increasingly ill, feverish and ranting. Morris again stays overnight with her not so much to ease her pain but fearful that her nocturnal ramblings will betray her involvement in her condition.

Don't wake the neighbours Mrs Medd!

Hold your tongue Mrs Medd!

Think of Irene Mrs Medd, locked in her bedroom.

By the Saturday Morris' vigil is over and he feels safe to leave the house. Medd appears to have made a dramatic recovery but one is aware of what they say about looks being deceiving. It is true that Medd was indeed sufficiently buoyed to take tea with a neighbour but the night would see her condition deteriorate so dramatically and so cruelly that there would be no way back. On the morning of Sunday 9 January 1927 she was discovered dead in her bed by her daughter Irene. Tests would later show that she had contracted a virulent form of septicaemia which left untreated had proved fatal.

Officially notified of the sudden death, Inspector Hodges and Detective Sergeant Puglsey of the Cardiff City police were called to 69 Stanway Road. These were seasoned officers and had arrived forearmed with a tip-off regarding the dead woman's association with Morris – a man whose reputation was not lost on them. He had long been a distant bogeyman whose involvement in the procurement of abortions had been implied in whispers but never made explicit. But here it was not only a baby who had perished. Whether acting on gut instinct or prior knowledge Pugsley diverted his gaze from the bedroom scene towards a patch of disturbed earth conspicuous in the newly laid out garden. Mere inches beneath a surface, hardened by the winter frost, the officers would uncover the pathetic body of a child, its body neatly, perhaps lovingly wrapped in a piece of cloth.

Discovery of baby in the garden

Morris was arrested in connection with the death of Medd by Detective Sergeant Pugsley as he returned home that afternoon. Though confronted by the policeman on his doorstep he put up little resistance. He probably knew that Medd's untimely death was inevitable. Informed by Pugsley that he had knowledge that he had been 'medically attending Hilda Medd', Morris' response was merely an enigmatic 'Least said, soonest mended'. Found in possession of a large quantity of tablets, he had been returning from the house of a Mrs Howells, a 'client' in Dogfield Street, Cathays.

The Ely Pied Piper

Who was this man for hire? This sordid Pied Piper secretly rewarded to spirit away dead infants of the city? The jury at his trial would learn that Morris was, perhaps surprisingly, a family man, married with three children residing in Holmesdale Street in Grangetown. Aged twenty-nine and a native son of Cardiff, he has served time abroad in the Army and claimed to have acquired grounding in massage whilst enlisted. Although now, on paper at least, a fitter's 'helper' he had enjoyed little honest employment and for the last twelve months been in receipt of unemployment pay. An air of public humiliation lingered over his cross-questioning at trial when the prisoner was asked to display to the court his uncalloused 'labourer's hands'. Describing himself as a 'physical culturalist', he had earned money in recent times as a jobbing masseur for various local amateur football teams. Whereas society at large may have accepted the relatively benign falsehood of his masseur's qualifications his purporting to be a 'doctor's assistant' was a far more unpalatable proposition. Morris had been all too pleased to inform his clients that he operated as the assistant to the respectable Dr Robert Longmore of Corporation Road. In reality, Morris was known to the good doctor merely as a patient of two years standing. Somewhat inevitably the fantasist had gained previous criminal convictions for 'false pretences' and gaining financial relief by 'false statements'.

A confession?

Morris was committed for trial at the following month's Assizes to be held at Cardiff. Having appeared before the magistrates on 10 January and duly returned to Cardiff Jail, Morris urged his captors to place him in a cell with another prisoner 'for company'. It would appear to have been a dreadful error of judgement on his part. His companion was to be Daniel Patrick Lyons, a young clerk from Haverford West who too awaited trial. What transpired between them would convict the abortionist. Foolish Morris; he so loved to talk about himself. His indiscreet chatter would betray him as something of a lady's man, 'women on the brain' according to Lyons. The disclosure that a fellow prisoner had dubbed him 'The Velvet handed

Sheik' brought a rare moment of mirth to those assembled in court. Lyons discovered his enforced associate to be a vain and conceited man, certain of his prowess. He spun the young clerk lurid tales of illegal medical operations that he had witnessed while in India. Lyons would later testify that 'when I tackled him as to his ability he told me a terrible tale'. He boasted to Lyons of having disposed of a baby by tossing it in to the Taff near the Windsor slipway. The child had been the product of an unholy union between a woman and her own adopted father. The gentleman, George Hunter, being of sound means, put up £1,200 to draw a veil over the episode only to see the hush money stolen by the woman's husband who used it to set up home with his mistress in Splott! Tangled web scarcely did it justice. It transpired that it was through a Rosie Richards, a friend of the baby's mother, that word of Morris and his work originally reached the ears of Hilda Medd.

The instigation of Lyons' statement here was absolutely crucial. If it were the case that the police had *interrogated* Lyons as a prisoner who had already been charged and awaiting trial then any evidence gleaned from it was inadmissible in court. Needless to say O Temple-Morris for the defence pushed hard for this interpretation. For the Crown it was asserted that not only had Morris asked to be paired with another man with whom he could chat, he himself had initiated the conversation and thus volunteered his own 'confession'. At no time, it was claimed had the police coerced Lyons into acting as an agent provocateur to extract information from Morris nor solicited a written transcript of their exchange. The judge, siding with the constabulary, found in favour of the prosecution. Lyons' testimony, validated as a purely voluntary gesture on his part, would stand.

The trial

Morris was lucky; he would not swing for his venal endeavours. Although the prosecution had prepared a murder charge it would be withdrawn due to lack of evidence. With the jury in turn completing the formality of returning a not guilty verdict to the capital charge Artemus Jones KC would move to one of manslaughter. The Crown case would now be one of 'procuring a miscarriage, by either giving (Hilda Medd) pills or through massaging'.

Morris' denial

Morris and his brief were vociferous in their 'comprehensive denial' of Lyons' testimony, all too aware of its magnitude. With little to lose and much to gain they would adopt a perilous strategy of questioning the integrity of Hodges and his investigating officers – a move guaranteed to alienate the police, judiciary and public alike. Magnanimously praising the valiant advocacy of the defence counsel, the judge wasted few words in condemning their undermining of their case:

> *By attempting to explain circumstances that otherwise seemed incapable of explanation by making charges of the gravest possible character against the police ... absolutely without foundation.*

Initially, Morris had asserted that Lyons had gleaned the 'facts' of the case from having brief sight of a copy of *The South Wales Echo* of 10 January while in custody. It was a mistake. The prosecution could and did easily prove that chronologically this was impossible and, furthermore the press reports had never made mention of the disposal of the Roberts' baby crucial to the Crown's case. On oath Morris admitted to inexplicably telling Lyons that, with regard to Hilda Medd's miscarriage he 'did not perform an illegal operation' *despite* not once being asked if he had. These errors were compounded by the cumulative effect of the many inconsistencies in Morris' recollection of the dates and times of meetings and conversation with key players in the squalid melodrama. Whether a liar tripping up over his own deceit or an innocent man disorientated by the weight of injustice is open to conjecture.

A fit-up?

Is it possible that Morris was set up by the police? The notion of a casually delivered 'confession' in a cell to a fellow prisoner may jar with a modern observer. One finds it hard to rationalise a scene in which a prisoner manages to first listen to a tale, memorise a host of names, dates and details only to leave the room, jot them down accurately and return. It must be borne in mind that as a clerk Lyons was presumably a man of reasonable education so we may be doing him and his mental skills a disservice. It is intriguing however that during the course of the trial Lyons would recall nuggets of incriminating information that were absent from his original statement much to the admiration of the prosecution team. Whatever the truth of the matter it is quite certain that the police could have done very little to further their case despite their possession of the facts without having the jury 'hear' them from the mouth of the accused. Would Morris' 'sensational adhoc disclosure' be so damning, so vital that the police Hodges and Pugsley may have manipulated the truth in order to create it?

There was more. A seemingly genuine client of Morris in his capacity as a masseur would give evidence as to his misguided medical ambition. He had called at the home of Mrs Edmunds in Wyndham Crescent on Christmas Eve 1926. He had cajoled the woman to let him have as a gift a 'surgical implement' that he had admired during a previous visit. Equally ominous was his borrowing of a medical textbook from Edmund's daughter.

O Temple Morris for the defence struggled to raise the spectre of uncertainty in the minds of the jury in his summing up but it was too little avail:

> *You must be satisfied that the chain of circumstantial evidence is forged beyond reasonable doubt. My submission is that without the evidence of Lyons there is not a scrap of evidence to say that this man is guilty of the crime of which he is charged. NOT A SCRAP!*

On Monday 21 February, the third day of the trial, Reginald Oliver Morris was found guilty of the manslaughter of Hilda Medd. He had induced her miscarriage by a 'combination of pills and physical manipulation' and left her in a condition that allowed infection to set in to which she succumbed. He was duly sentenced. 'Four years for an amateur masseur' as the headline in the next day's *Western Mail* succinctly put it.

To the end Morris insisted that he had no knowledge of Medd's miscarriage although his near permanent residency at her house during the last week of her life made a mockery of his claim. His initial manoeuvre had been to suggest that Medd herself must have buried the infant's body, though in court Dr O'Driscoll made it clear that during the final days of her life she would have been barely capable of walking let alone lifting a spade in the garden. Morris subsequently proffered the name of Mr Leyshon. He was a travelling salesman dealing in sewing machines apparently on intimate terms with Medd. Could it have been he who fathered her child? Morris also accused Leyshon of the continual supply of drugs to Medd. Whatever the extent of his alleged complicity in the crime his role in the harrowing melee was never expounded in court.

The defendant had made many contacts on the seedy fringes of the medical world or, rather those seeking some covert assistance. Whether Morris had simply seized an opportunity to supplement his meagre income, offered a service and grown accustomed to its financial rewards one shall never know. He had not meant to cause Medd's death but little sympathy for his subsequent judicial plight can be felt. He was a blight on society, a nuisance whose meddling was both illegal and potentially lethal. The emphatic closing statement by Artemus Jones KC for the prosecution would crystallise the public's feeling toward such a man and his sordid trade:

It is of vital importance to the community that women should not be subjected to the illegal practices of the kind suggested in this case. Unlawful acts of this kind always take place secretly since the people involved in them knew that they are wrong. That was why we have to rely on circumstantial evidence to convict.

The Offences Against The Person Act had been on the statute book since 1861. Section 58 made abortion a criminal offence even if undertaken on medical grounds. The tariff was three years to life. Only two years after Morris' conviction the Infant Life Preservation Act would decriminalise a termination in exceptional cases in which there was severe jeopardy to the mother's health. Despite the formation of the Abortion Law Reform Association in 1936 it would be 1967 before the act of 1861 was repealed. It would not legalise abortion but firmly placed the decision to act in the hands of the doctor.

Chapter 10

The Horrific Killing of Stephen Gilbert Roath
1936

o all intents and purposes Stephen Gilbert appeared a model citizen. In Cardiff he played the role of popular shopkeeper, a quiet man with a loving wife. In his native Pontypridd, where he visited weekly, he was a devoted church goer and pillar of the local community in which his family enjoyed a certain social standing. But the wretchedly violent death of Gilbert would shatter this façade of respectability and see the conundrum of his life laid bare with the spirals of suspicion and confusion leading the Cardiff police a merry dance – and ultimately – to failure.

The inquest/murder scene

Stephen Gilbert, aged forty-two, was found dead around 1pm on the afternoon of Sunday 7 June 1936. His body lay face down on the floor of his stockroom at the rear of his green-grocer's shop located on the corner of Croft Street and Clive Place in the Roath area of the city. The victim of a frenzied attack, there were at least forty lacerations to his head, neck, face and arms. His blood decorated the close confines of the room. His killer has certainly come equipped to commit the crime. It was agreed by Dr Buist the police surgeon and consultant pathologist Dr Harold Scholberg that the first bone shattering blows to the face had been delivered by means of a knuckleduster. Then, whilst reeling, a multitude of vicious strikes by a metal rod had perforated his head with wounds. It

The junction of Croft Street and Clive Place today. Although now residential the building's commercial past is still apparent. The original entrance to Gilbert's shop is the blocked doorway at the centre of picture. The author

was recorded that his face had been 'mutilated beyond all recognition'. The body had been partially covered with sheets of brown wrapping paper. Much of the detail of the scene was suppressed in contemporary newspaper reports and for good reason. Such was the severity of his beating and subsequent blood loss that a pool of it had formed in the cellar below. It had dripped overnight through the upstairs floorboards. The sight of this grisly accumulation was enough to cause one young policeman to vomit on the spot. With the attack timed at around 10pm the previous night it was pitifully certain that over the course of just two hours Gilbert had collapsed and agonizingly bled to death after staggering around the room.

Such was the rush of determination that heralded the launch of the manhunt that its first four days would see some officers working gruelling fourteen and twenty hour shifts. For the first time in Cardiff policing officers would employ a 'fanning out' method to trawl for clues; an operation recently introduced by the Metropolitan force to great effect. Teams would radiate out from the murder scene in concentric circles making house to house calls and searching for the murder weapon. Despite concentrated effort their hard work would prove less than fruitful. A senior officer would later confess that the first seven days on the case were 'a week of near unremitting toil'.

The shopkeeper had in life been a neat, fastidious somewhat inconsequential little man but it was now strikingly apparent that someone had wanted him dead and had revelled in its viciously sadistic execution. Despite a sum of missing money the police knew that robbery was not the true motive for the murder. The 'tangled skein of evidence' would prove quite baffling. J A Wilson, Cardiff's Chief Constable, would soon cryptically concede that:

The crime [had] brought to light many things that the police did not know about this apparently respectable grocer and, it is this aspect of his life that is making the solution all the more difficult.

At this early stage Wilson was yet to realise how so very accurate and such a curse his judgement would be.

The murderer had the briefest window of opportunity. Gilbert's errand boy had left the shop at exactly 9.15pm. It was assumed that the killer had lain in wait for his departure which shortly followed that of the female shop assistant. He then immediately approached the front door and knocked to gain entry. *Crucially* the murder had been committed in a private part of the premises separated from the retail area. There was no way that Gilbert would have allowed anyone entry to the shop and then his storeroom after closing time if he had not been comfortable with their being there. It begged the question of Gilbert knowing his killer. When the body was discovered the next day none of the electric lights were on nor, according to the neighbours, had they been at any time during the night. With dusk timed at around 10pm on the Saturday it meant that the killer had a mere thirty minutes of daylight to gain entrance, kill and leave. It was deduced that it would have been impossible for him to commit his ghastly act and its aftermath in darkness, the small storeroom window offering the merest glimpse of illumination by the street lights.

Local man

Police were convinced that only a local man or a close associate of Gilbert would have been savvy to the shopkeeper's fastidious weekend closing routine. In the busy, densely populated street an outsider would have been acutely conspicuous in any attempt to case the shop over the period necessary to build up a picture of Gilbert's movements. Yet a mysterious stranger did exist. Half a dozen corroborated reports described a well-dressed man in his early twenties pacing the pavement on the corner of Croft Street and its junction with Elm Street. It would have been a perfect vantage point for anyone to observe Gilbert's premises from a distance. Did he cross the road towards the shop? Nobody saw him do so. Perhaps he was a lookout. He was certainly there at the crucial time. In line with the atmosphere of defeat that would dog the whole murder enquiry concerted attempts failed to trace the dapper man.

Leaving the shop and discovery

The last person to see Gilbert alive was William Cotty, a schoolboy whom he employed to run errands. As was customary the lad left the shop at 9.15pm shutting the door behind him. Gilbert was thus sealed within; the securely Yale locked front door the only point of entry and departure. When he had failed to return to their home in Cottrell Road as expected that Saturday night his wife Nellie was not unduly alarmed. Perhaps accustomed to his nocturnal habits she would later claim that she supposed that he had decided to spend the night with his brother in Ponypridd. But his non appearance by the Sunday lunchtime however was of concern enough to ask a boy to walk the short journey to the shop to take a look. Returning with the news that the door was locked but the bar missing she decided that she must take a look for herself. Just able to ascertain the prostate form of her husband through the tiny Clive Place window her horrified screams drew the Winton's son from his family's upstairs flat. Begging him through tears to breakdown the shop door the petrified lad refused. An anxious call to the police would within minutes alert officers to the scene who would make light work of the grocer's locked front door.

The Gilbert's family home in Cottrell Road seen today. The author

Despite the horrific beating and chaotic scene within the shop only one witness claimed to hear anything suspicious that night. A cyclist riding up Clive Place alongside Gilbert's storeroom testified to hearing a distant 'oh!' emanating from within. This was timed at approximately 10.25pm. If it *were* Gilbert's agonising cry it was quite likely his first and last utterance made during the course of his savage ordeal. A jaw broken swiftly in several places would have put paid to that. Perhaps surprisingly the Winton family living above the shop heard nothing untoward that night as did John Tull the proprietor of the fish and chip shop next door. It was even accepted that for at least part of the time that the killer busied himself with Gilbert's demise a group of youths had sat chatting on the ledge outside the shop front. They would also testify to hearing nothing. Gilbert's gruesome death would pass unnoticed by the world outside his window.

A costly mistake

Acknowledging the loss of momentum in the investigation a bullish police spokesman vowed that the murder would not go

The rear of the shop along Clive Place is now a separate address. It was here that that Gilbert's battered and bloody corpse was discovered. The author

down as another 'unsolved'. Defiant in the face of the odds insiders knew that the trail had gone cold. With the benefit of hindsight it was true that the police had lost potentially crucial hours in the investigation and criticism of this 'mistake' was wounding. At around 10pm on the night of the slaying PC George Howcroft out on a routine patrol noticed that the bar across Gilbert's shop door was inexplicably absent. With no answer downstairs he succeeded in rousing the occupants of the flat above. When asked, the resident Winton sisters were unsure of the number of the grocer's home in nearby Cottrell Road. Discouraged by their uncertainty and satisfied that the door was secure he carried on his way. It was after all not his duty to locate the proprietor's home address. At that very moment Gilbert lay inside battered but still alive while his killer hid mere yards away. With this chance spurned to steal a march on their quarry Cardiff constabulary would repent at their leisure.

Finding the weapon and wallet

A breakthrough came on 8 June in Bedford Lane, no more than 500 yards away on the other side of City Road, Gilbert's wallet and an iron bar were found together. Believing it to be the murder weapon, the police issued a photograph of the object. Measuring nearly 14 inches long, with flaking remains of blue paint, it was assumed to have originally been part of a lorry's tail gate. True to form the appeal to trace the whereabouts of that vehicle was still born. The location of the bar was crucial and added credence to the investigators' judgement that the killer was a local man. Bedford Lane appeared to all but the cognoscenti as a cul-de-sac and no one unaware of its true course would choose it as an escape route, blood stained and mere minutes after committing murder. For the police their quarry was not just a Cardiff man he was a Roath man; living less than quarter of a mile from the scene of his crime. If anything in this case could be 'known', Detective Inspector Lewis knew that the killer had not fled; he lived close by and was being skilfully shielded by his confederates. It would prove a galling prospect for the investigating team.

Here was the dreadful paradox. Precisely *because* he was a local man no one reported seeing him (them?) in the vicinity. His presence in the street was in no way remarkable. He was a friend, neighbour perhaps relative of those passing by. And the passers by must have been plentiful. This after all was a warm summer's Saturday night. That section of Croft Street connects two popular public houses with a fish and chip shop in the middle. This is to say nothing of the density of population in an area of cheek by jowl terraced houses.

Too many leads
The police soon found that credible theories surrounding Gilbert's death were legion. It had become the nightmare scenario for the investigating team; just too many leads, too many possibilities. Each, however tenuous, had to be diligently pursued. With each deadend sapping morale and eating up man hours, the team found themselves diverted from the line of enquiry that may just be 'The One'. An early sojourn to the Rhondda following a tip-off yielded nothing. Knowing that the assailant must have been covered in his victim's blood an urgent plea called for the public to search for discarded clothing heavily bloodstained. Fevered activity around the city quickly

centred on a section of Plymouth Great Wood in Ely. Whatever had been discovered there was soon discounted by the police.

Entering the second week of the murder hunt the police were no further in their hunt for the killer. An impatient public were vociferous in their scorn for the perceived impotence of the murder investigation. Through the pages of the press a popular clamour arose to 'call in the Yard'. The evocation of the name of the mighty London police headquarters the then voguish response to any 'failing' provincial force. A proud Cardiff Constabulary would have none of it. The team under the direction of the dynamic Detective Inspector Lewis were angry and they would let the people know. They believed it was the public's apathy that lay at the root of the problem with their disinterest and lack of cooperation that had hindered the murder hunt from the outset. The police would also choose to vent their spleen in the pages of the press. Explicit articles in the *Western Mail* emphasised the public's responsibility as the 'eyes and ears' of the city to come forward with any information they had. Not too subtly the law in regard to the withholding of evidence was printed for all to see. If the public wanted justice then they themselves had need to work for it. A police spokesman was quoted at length as to his colleagues' awareness of the fickle nature of the populous 'after the first rush of grief and public sympathy had ebbed'. The balance of responsibility had shifted. It could be construed that police had washed their hands of the problem and now laid it firmly at the feet of the citizens. It had descended into a war of attrition; the police seemingly pitted against both the fugitive killer *and* the public at large.

With the best intentions a £100 reward put up by the *Echo & Western Mail* sought to cajole a response from an indifferent readership. However, what was devised as a means of mining precious nuggets of information played out as little more than a test of the public's imagination. The Western Mail offices were bombarded with correspondence detailing outlandish theories and complex murder scenarios many, it was said, as ingenious as any of the famous Edgar Wallace literary mysteries. The police had no need of a legion of armchair detectives and were rightly disappointed by the results. To the investigators' chagrin among the hundreds of signed letters received were dozens of anonymous contributions. More infuriating still that several of these untraceable writers were judged to have alluded to 'significant items of interest' with direct bearing on the case that the police felt their authors were fearful to expand upon. Through gritted teeth an unnamed senior detective divulged to the press:

The facts are like an empty suit of clothes waiting for their owner, who, once found will fit them perfectly. I know as much of this man as of any man on whose trail I have ever worked, and I know, as I have always known that I am near to him and that I will ultimately get him, if someone does not get him before me.

Money, gambling and sex

Gilbert had found himself in the position of being financially well off with a secret addiction to gambling and sex. The ability now to pay for his pleasures would prove a dangerous lure draining both his conscience and his bank account. Unbeknown to his siblings, Gilbert had obtained 500 gold sovereigns from their mother's house after her death. He had wasted little time into converting them into £800 cash; a tidy nest egg in mid 1930s Cardiff. A new, detached villa in the smart suburbs would set one back only £650. With this windfall secret from the family the animosity between Gilbert and them derived from him, as executor and main beneficiary to her will, vetoing their plans to liquidate some family property. Gilbert, unlike siblings, now of course had the luxury of holding out for a better price. Despite this rift cordial relations were to remain strained but intact between the brothers and sisters. By the time of his death Gilbert had owned the shops for only five months having previously managed it for several years. Needing to pay former owner Mr King in instalments for the premises and stock he admitted to a few business associates that he was 'broke', his 'inheritance' summarily frittered away. The inquest into his death would spotlight a predilection for betting that had cost him at least £10 a day. For the last three years a friend, Sarah Hartwell of Oxford Street, had called into his premises to place bets on his behalf. She herself had been in the shop during the lunchtime on the day of his death. Although a spendthrift the busy shop had kept him afloat. It was reckoned that on a good Saturday Gilbert could take up to £90 over the counter and his killer had made off with this sum and the unknown amount in his wallet.

Rumours and sexual assault?

Wild rumours began to circulate in the locality and with each passing day a new theory was born more lurid than the last. As the local press put it 'the tongue of scandal had sharpened its keen edge on many innocent people'. Gilbert's corner shop became the focus of intense scrutiny by locals and tram-transported visitors alike. On numerous occasions constables were distracted from their primary duties to hold back the crowds and clear the narrow thoroughfare for official vehicles such was the scrum of morbid sightseers. Amid this confusion of theories senior detectives privately dismissed the notion of a sexual assault on Gilbert and this aspect of their enquiries was closely shielded from the press. They felt that the crude interference with the shopkeeper's clothes was a cynical ruse by the killer to feign a violent homosexual encounter and planned to disorientate an investigation from the outset. But in the course of enquiries evidence *had* transpired which linked Gilbert to the fringes of the secretive homosexual milieu in the city. Armed with this revelation the police were agonisingly obliged to pursue this avenue of enquiry even though such a premise had been officially discounted. Such was the desperation not to miss a single clue the team still found them wasting valuable time bringing in and questioning known 'deviants' to no avail.

Connections and speculation

Speculation increased regarding Gilbert having a week prior been the victim of a night time attack by a group of men near Waterloo Gardens in Roath. Newspaper reports described a man being set upon by four unknown men whom had trailed him in a car. The unnamed victim's terrified cries for help alerted both local residents and forced his attackers to flee. Very serious consideration was given to Gilbert being the victim of this assault. Was the curtailed beating a warning of some sort and directly related to his death? Another possible lead faded from view when it was established beyond doubt that Gilbert had been in Pontypridd in the company of his sister on the night in question. Gilbert *had* however recently sustained injuries in what was an extraordinary event. On Good Friday last he was the most seriously injured of a group who fell from the draw-bridge of Castell Coch when it collapsed in a freak accident. The more superstitious of folk may have viewed it as prescient warning.

On 22 June, two weeks after Gilbert's murder a 'sensational development' would rock the investigation and the local press. Quite incredibly, 'Ianto' Jones, a twenty-year-old from Tonypany, had voluntarily confessed to the murder of the shopkeeper while being held at Brixton Prison on an unrelated burglary charge. Detective Inspector Lewis, head of Cardiff CID and his men would barely contain their relief and excitement at the news. Lewis himself vowed to travel to make the arrest and return Jones to Cardiff. It would prove a dreadful and humiliating mis-judgement. In reality Ianto Jones' innocence was unequivocal – he was not even in Wales at the time of Gilbert's death. A routine double checking of the suspect's statement as to his movements on the night in question would have proved it. The excitement and triumphalism surrounding the arrest – *any arrest*, had inexcusably blinded investigators to the facts. It was sadly fitting that their misguided endeavour would end in fiasco. With the pair of Cardiff detectives sent to retrieve him from London, Jones, having inexplicably confessed to the crime, would turn the tables on his captors. In a split second with the accompanying police officers momentarily distracted en route from Paddington, their prisoner recklessly flung himself through the open window of the speeding express train in an insane bid for freedom. He was found injured and exhausted some two hours later by farm workers, the fugitive hiding up a tree in the countryside near Caerwent. He has risked his life to fulfil a fantasy. It had been a pointless and futile gesture by a simple, uneducated petty thief by which he gained the moment of notoriety for which he craved. Ultimately, only charged and convicted of wasting police time, the episode would do irreparable damage to the psyche of the Cardiff police and expectant public alike. The investigation would not recover from this devastating yet wholly avoidable setback.

There are a myriad of overlapping theories regarding the murder of Stephen Gilbert. All pursued, none proved or disproved. His death was certainly not the result of a simple robbery gone wrong. Was it fear or friendship that opened his door to his killer? Although in dispute with his family their squabble could never countenance such a revenge. Did a rogue bookmaker employ an enforcer to call in a gambling debt? Surely the installation of fear not cold-blooded murder is the key to a man's wallet. Blackmail? With his longing for illicit sexual encounters could a fellow brothel habitué have grasped an opportunity to extort money from a prosperous local shop keeper? Again, the golden goose dead is worthless. There is the matter of his alleged homosexual dalliances, then of course a serious criminal offence. Again a blackmail scenario seems the logical outcome rather than murder, the police themselves condemning the partial stripping of the body as a ruse. If one denounces the negligible possibility that his murder was a purely random attack by person or persons unknown to the victim then the most likely motive was that of revenge. Jealousy is a corrosive emotion. There were believed to be a host of secret female friends of the deceased. It only took one husband or boyfriend hell bent on retribution. This was murder as punishment and humiliation and a score settled by a man with psychopathic tendencies. Perhaps Gilbert had simply taken up with the wrong girl and paid a dreadful price for his mistake.

It transpired that the lascivious Gilbert had endured sleepless nights after an affair with a particular female acquaintance had been exposed. Five months prior to his death he had confided in Thomas Fearnly, a friend in the motor trade, that he genuinely feared for his life because of his transgression; 'messing about with another woman' as he put it. A somewhat incredulous Fearnly would soon see for himself Gilbert's fear made flesh. One afternoon in the grocer's shop the two men chatted about the woman in question and moreover the fear of her boyfriend's wrath. A cautious Gilbert was careful not to divulge her name even to his friend. Remarkably, as if summoning up the devil the very woman walked through the doorway from the street. A palpably shaken Gilbert stood rooted to the spot mouthing only a shocked 'That's her!' to the other man. With a cheery 'Hello Steve! How are you?' the woman approached the counter. Fearnly later described her as a strikingly attractive lady in her late thirties. A redhead in fashionable attire, she was certainly the type capable of turning a man's head. The awkward silence that followed encouraged Fearnly to bid the couple farewell and leave. He would never see the woman nor hear Gilbert refer to their clandestine relationship again. Here was a motive, a witness and possible protagonist. What price the mysterious redhead's identity? Possibly the one vital piece of the jigsaw that could make sense of their endless hours of graft. Incredibly not one person came forward with a positive lead as to the woman's name or whereabouts. It seemed inconceivable that the description of such a memorable woman could have failed to be recognised by anyone in Cardiff but not one positive lead resulted from this important line of enquiry. The redhead had faded from view.

The inquest into Gilbert's death took place towards the end of July 1936 over a period of three days. His death had truly overturned a stone and the people of Cardiff enthusiastically turned up on mass to be disgusted by what had crawled from underneath. Presided over by the City Coroner, Gerald Tudor, the jury found no need to retire to consider their verdict. It was all too obvious; wilful murder by person or persons unknown.

Over 3,000 people were interviewed over the course of the investigation with nearly 400 written statements taken. At the close of the inquest the Cardiff police were at great pains to stress that their enquiries had not nor would not cease but, in reality, the murder hunt had slowly wound down to nothing; a cue for the recriminations over their failure to begin. The continual see-saw between expectation and disappointment and the impenetrable layers of Gilbert's life had succeeded in confounding the Cardiff Constabulary.

For a case as perplexing as this it is quite fitting that it warrants an equally enigmatic postscript. Was it true that as far back as the third day of the initial investigation the police had interviewed a man whom over two years later would become their prime suspect? In June 1936 a labourer had undergone routine questioning in regard to his whereabouts on the night of Gilbert's death. His story of drinking in the *Crofts Hotel* had satisfied his interrogators and his transcription duly logged and filed. However, the appearance of this man's wife at the Cardiff Law Courts in the summer of 1938 was deemed important enough to reopen the case which had all the while lain dormant. The couple's relationship had broken down and the wife had dark secrets to tell. Her husband was a violent drunk, well versed in subterfuge and deception. A petty criminal he was known to Gilbert and had broken into his shop on at least one occasion. On the night of Gilbert's murder her husband had actually returned home around 2am – a fact corroborated by their lodger. The following morning it was quite obvious that he had washed and dried his clothes worn the night before. His manner evasive and actions erratic he had been observed by the lodger hiding a package behind his green-house in the garden. The local gossip in regard to Gilbert's death became a cause of extreme agitation to him.

Now with sufficient reason to call in their man the police would re-question the suspect some two years after his first inter-view. Conspicuously anxious, the labourer would contradict his statement of June 1936. He now admitted to leaving the public house that night only to frequent a well known brothel in the Riverside area of the city. Returning home to Roath around 1.30am, he swore to not knowing the name of his recent female companion. His use of prostitutes was crucial. Police had recently gathered evidence that the man had, prior to Gilbert's murder, boasted to drinking cronies of his knowledge of the shopkeeper's sexual proclivities and how he had on several occasions made his acquaintance while walking the streets in the early hours. Investigators theorised that the labourer's previous breaking in to Gilbert's shop was a test of courage, his ultimate aim being blackmail. The shopkeeper was seen as a cash cow to be milked in turn for the labourer's silence as to their mutual 'friends'. The suspect was indeed known to be privy to the gossip surrounding Gilbert's 'inheritance'. Although kept low key at the time many senior detectives were convinced that they had finally found their man but he would never be brought to trial. With the lodger's incriminating evidence deemed insubstantial the notion of the labourer's guilt rested solely with his wife. The bitter irony of finally having a witness who was prepared to speak but whose word was inadmissible was not lost on the investigating officers. A wife could not testify against her husband other than in extraordinary circumstances – this was not one. And so here would it all end. The file on the horrific death of Stephen Gilbert was once more placed on the shelf – his murderer not convicted but perhaps the crime *not* unsolved.

Chapter 11

Love is a tyrant ...
Joan Canham and Ronald
Lewis
Cardiff
1951 and 1947

Love is a tyrant; it darkens the reason, confounds discretion. Deaf to counsel, it runs a headlong course to desperate madness.

> H Edmund Davies QC for the defence quoting
> John Ford in the trial of Donald John Bowling,
> 2 April 1952

Love is such a dangerous thing. It can manifest itself in many ways. When things go wrong, a relationship once kind and forgiving can be ruined by jealousy and spite. The desire to have and to hold is consumed by the need to covert and possess – maybe even destroy. In its rawest state it is wholly oblivious to propriety. In the blink of an eye it may lead one into danger, to lie, to cheat and conceal. The fury of the 'scorned' is not only felt by the female of the species. Could it also precipitate a horror or be complicit in its covering up? Within the following two short accounts the grave consequences of a twisted love can be gauged.

Joan Canham

Cardiff in 1951 and a domestic tragedy that would needlessly shatter two young lives. Joan Canham never lived beyond the age of nineteen. A strikingly pretty and vivacious young lady, she was employed as a clerk at the St Mary Street offices of the Cooperative Wholesale Society. Like most girls of her age her

Joan Canham, the tragic victim of falling out of love.
Author's collection

life revolved around the cinema and dancehall. For the past two years she had been courted by Donald John Bowling, an apprentice fitter from Percy Street in Grangetown, one year her senior. The couple had grown close, with tentative plans for their engagement during the forthcoming Christmas period. However, for reasons not known, the young man would fall out of favour during October 1951 and Joan broke off all contact. Bowling was devastated and bombarded his former sweetheart with calls begging her if not for a reconciliation then at least to meet and talk things through.

Initially reticent, Joan would relent, agreeing for Bowling to meet her from work on the afternoon of 8 November 1951. Escorting her home by bus to Cathays, it was clear that Bowling was a troubled soul. Consumed by jealousy prompted by rumours of a blossoming romance between Joan and a new suitor he questioned her relentlessly. Joan's explanations did little to appease him. By now standing outside her home at 68 Gelligaer Street the tone of their conversation would darken. Joan allegedly laughed at Bowling's proposals to reunite and scorned his begging for a second chance. This perceived 'sneering' would have grave ramifications.

It could be said Bowling had a predicilition for knives. Earlier that day en route to meeting Joan he had purchased a large sheath knife from John Hall (Tools) Ltd. It was double edged and deadly. It was secreted on his person throughout. He would later claim that he had bought it, in his words to 'bluff' Joan. It would in fact kill her.

Maybe alerted to something in his speech or simply to draw their conversation to a close Joan made the error of stepping towards Bowling before retreating through her front door. Without warning her former beau pushed the dreadful blade over five inches deep into her stomach. Reeling backwards into

The Gelligaer Street home of Joan Canham seen today. The author

her house and the arms of her mother, Joan's blood loss was rapid and heavy.

Bowling panicked. Later criticised for not aiding the stricken girl, he instead ran all the way to the Central Police Station. Laying the bloodstained knife on the desk, he confessed to the stabbing of Joan. Meanwhile his sweetheart was being transferred from St David's Hospital to the Infirmary whose superior facilities would be her only chance of survival. The doctors and surgeons in attendance fought a losing battle.

During the night her condition plummeted and all concerned knew that her end was near. The police, with their prisoner Bowling summoned to the hospital, an extraordinary bedside court was convened. Shielded by screens and attached to a transfusion machine, Joan would give a breathless yet coherent testimony. At one point even Bowling himself was permitted to question the girl. So overcome was he that smelling salts were required to revive him. At the later trial it was found that much of her words had been mistranscribed. The stenographer was partially deaf and impeded by both Joan's weak utterances and the hum of hospital machinery. Those at her bed had heard clear enough though. Her words read back to her Joan marked her deposition with an 'X', too weak to sign her name. At 2.50am, about half an hour later, she passed away, surrounded by her family.

Bowling was charged with murder and ordered to stand trial at the Glamorgan Assizes held in Cardiff in April 1952. Entering a plea of 'not guilty', he would maintain throughout that he had not planned to harm Joan but merely frighten her. How this 'fear' would rekindle their romance was never made clear. His version of events would have Joan accidentally brushing against the blade in a manner quite extraordinary in the light of her grievous wound. In addition, the prosecution highlighted Bowling's confessing to his 'stabbing' of Joan – a strangely inappropriate word for someone claiming that her wound derived from an 'accidental encounter'.

Many believed that his 'love' for Joan had bordered on obsession. Much was made of Bowling's otherwise spotless character with colleagues and friends vouching for him. In the end it would be Edmund Davies' impassioned oratory in defence of his client that proved boldly effective. In a clear display of mercy, despite the judge's warning to the contrary, the jury found Bowling guilty of the lesser charge of manslaughter, sentencing him to five years' imprisonment.

Ronald Lewis

Cardiff in 1947 and a dangerous liaison at the water's edge?

Around 1pm on 31 May 1947 two local boys would discover a corpse in the Taff near to the Sophia Gardens side of Canton Bridge. The dead man was named as thirty-six-year-old Ronald Lewis a GWR platelayer from Morganstown. It was immediately clear that the man had met his death the night before. Having sustained some nasty head injuries obviously not self inflicted the police would open a murder investigation and attempt to piece together the man's last known movements and how he was to find himself in the park.

The forensic lab would deduce that the damage to Lewis's face was a product of a series of vicious punches delivered by a powerful man. None, however, had been sufficient to have directly caused his death. Ronald Lewis had perished by

*Sophia Gardens looking towards Canton (aka Cardiff) Bridge. Ronald Lewis'
body was discovered on the muddy bank of the Taff approximately in line with the
tree in the centre of picture.* The author

drowning. Lungs horrifically clogged with riverbank mud, he
had laid facedown and unconscious at the water's edge. The
question now was how he had entered the river. Possibly thrown
or knocked in by his opponent, it was equally viable that,
awakening some time later, dazed and confused from his savage
beating the unfortunate Lewis had accidentally stumbled into
the Taff. Two significant pools of his blood had collected on
dry land some twenty feet from where he was found, suggesting
that he had been prostrate on the grass for a period.

Although his wristwatch was missing, presumably submerged
in the Taff, his wallet was intact in his pocket. Thus, with the
most likely motive of robbery dismissed the police would labour
hard to ascertain not how but *why* he had met his death. The
park after dark was the haunt of courting couples and furtive
assignations and the police worked on the assumption that
Lewis had perhaps been taken for a 'peeping tom' or was himself
involved in an illicit tryst. Did a moonlit meeting turn sour? A

witness passing on the bridge that night would testify to seeing a couple at or very near the spot that his body was located.

Despite the police trawling city centre public houses for a clue to any associate that the deceased might have had that night the case would remain hampered by a lack of evidence. He was known to have frequented various pubs on the evening of his death. Work colleagues were under the impression that Lewis had travelled into town to celebrate his birthday. Another credible theory had him in the city centre innocently running an errand for a friend. Some believed that bachelor Lewis was out that evening specifically seeking female companionship. Needless to say any of the possible scenarios were far from being mutually exclusive. Police appeals to any doctor or chemist to come forward that may have treated Lewis' opponent's injuries would come to naught.

Enter the enigmatic 'Mrs S'. The Cardiff police managed to locate a vital witness to that evening's mellee but her recollections would prove frustratingly treacherous. She at first claimed that she was indeed with Lewis in the park that evening where an altercation ensued between him and man called Wilson who was also known to her. This was later contradicted by a subsequent claim that she had been with a different male companion and together saw Lewis involved in a brawl with a third man. Under police pressure her account ultimately changed to that of her being alone and witnessing a burly man unknown to her assaulting Lewis somewhere in the distance. The vital fact here was that 'Mrs S' had not only been irrefutably acquainted with the victim but they had previously enjoyed each other's company in that very park. The police were perhaps justifiably convinced that the woman held the key to the killer's identity but her fear had got the better of her. The sudden arrival of her sailor husband back in Cardiff would be sufficient to still her once wagging tongue. The gregarious 'Mrs S' would fall forever silent and disappear from the investigation if not the dark thoughts of the officers involved.

All other leads were to go nowhere. With the trail as cold as the victim's waterlogged body the bizarre death of Ronald Lewis would remain unsolved. With the lack of a definitive reason for Lewis being in the park that night or any substantiated clue to his attacker's identity or motivation, on 29 August 1947 an open verdict was recorded. Perhaps his friend's opinion of Lewis recorded at the inquest should serve as an ambiguous epitaph:

> *An easy going sort of chap. Matey with everyone and anyone with no particular attachments.*

Perhaps it's prudent to chose one's 'mates' wisely.

Chapter 12

Carnage at Pear Tree Cottage: Ruby Carter Penlline 1960

It must surely be one of the most dreadful of crimes by which you set out to harm those whom love and trust you unquestioningly. With all morality and compassion left far behind what must it be like to look in their terrified eyes and ignore their cries for mercy? The protector turned persecutor.

2 January 1960. In the Vale of Glamorgan the village of Penlline, near Cowbridge, stood Pear Tree Cottage, a pretty but unremarkable rural dwelling. But behind its neatly painted green door lay a gruesome secret. The upstairs bedroom had been transformed into a scene of abject carnage. Ruby Carter aged thirty-three lay dead on her blood-soaked bed having been brutally battered to death. With her face beaten to a pulp with a heavy iron bar, the ferocity of the attack was such that an arc of sprayed gore coated the walls and ceiling. She had been five months pregnant. But further barbarity was apparent. Curled up in the opposite corner of the room lay her six-year-old son Alun, suffering severe head injuries and barely clinging to life.

The tragic pair had been discovered by their husband and father, thirty-three-year-old Evan George Carter, returning home after a long shift in the nearby Aberthaw asbestos plant. They had been married some eight years. Carter claimed that knowing his wife was beyond help, he immediately bundled up his stricken child and drove him to his parents' Cowbridge home. Only later would he notify the police. With Bridgend Hospital lacking the appropriate facilities the critically injured Alun was transferred to Morriston in Swansea for intensive care. His father would visit him daily. All the while, Carter continued to cut a pitiful figure – a model of dignified stoicism attempting to deal with his devastating loss. What the neighbours did not know but the police strongly suspected was that Carter himself had committed the ghastly assault and murder of his kith and kin.

During the first few weeks after the slaying a widespread panic enveloped the rural areas of the Vale so isolated after nightfall. The locals were not to know that the killer was indeed one of their own and currently benefiting from their sympathy rather than suspicion. The grieving husband even had the temerity to pen a column in the popular *Empire News* Sunday newspaper in which he acknowledged public scepticism about him and decried the 'wicked gossips ... bandying' his name about. In a cloying piece entitled 'A murdered girl's husband speaks – I never knew a man could hurt so much', Carter would present himself as a devoted family man in lucrative employment so much looking forward to the birth of his second child. Snapshots from the family album would lend a ghoulish touch.

From the outset the team, led by Detective T Williams, head of Glamorgan CID, were unconvinced as to the robbery that

had at least *appeared* to have taken place at the cottage precipitating the death of Ruby Carter. There were far two many unanswered questions here. Why had the front door been left unlocked in the morning? With £35 missing the thief would have to have known precisely where the cash had been painstakingly hidden. Jewellery clearly displayed had

In the wake of the brutal murder of his wife Carter would protest his innocence to all and sundry. Author's collection

Ruby and Carter at the time of their wedding. Author's collection

been left untouched. Why indeed would an opportunist thief enter a bedroom and savagely batter a sleeping woman to death?

These were vast improbabilities but it would be local expertise in forensic science that would ultimately prove Carter's downfall. Running tests at the Home Office laboratories in Llanishen, Senior Forensic Officer Brian Morgan would deduce that the pin-head sized specks of blood on Carter's jacket and trousers worn on the day of the murder were almost certainly caused by the spray generated by striking his wife's open wounds. Furthermore, the marks on his raincoat were consistent with having held the bloody murder weapon close for a period of time. The suspected murder weapon itself, a type of iron 'knocker' bar, when eventually recovered would also test positive when tested for exposure to blood.

His arrest on Friday 15 January at a stroke transformed Carter from victim to cowardly murderer. A month later, while held in the cell at Cowbridge Police Station, the bombshell of an apparent and frankly inexplicable confession to a young constable would prove a revelation at his trial at the Glamorgan

Pear Tree Cottage in the sleepy village of Penlline flanked by policemen in the wake of the brutal murder of its female occupant. Author's collection

Assizes. Without prompting, in the midst of small talk Carter was quoted as saying: 'Yesterday was a better day for me with the outside witnesses. I have to *say* that I didn't do it but they can prove it.'

With the jury temporarily dismissed, legal argument raged as to its validity. With the judge ruling that it was indeed admissible in court it proved a devastating blow to his defence.

His image as a devoted family man destroyed the prosecution were to paint a picture of a man at his wit's end from the worry of debt and the cost of yet another mouth to feed. Despite strong rebuttals from his family in particular this would form the central plank behind the theory of Carter's true motivation to kill. Mr Justice Richards for the defence was to make little head way with his questioning of the relatively small amount of bloodstains found on the accused or the possibility that the contamination was in fact caused by Carter ministering to his injured son.

On Monday 28 March, after a mere half hour's deliberation, Evan George Carter was found guilty of the wilful murder of his wife. A pitiful whispered 'No' was the sole reply to the clerk's question to the accused as to whether there was any reason sentence should not be passed upon him. Mr Justice Barry on 'very clear evidence of this terrible crime' handed down a life term ordering the prisoner to be transported forthwith to be detained at Cardiff Prison. Around two months earlier in his column in the *Empire News* Carter had written: 'Whoever killed my wife must be a raving maniac and all I hope is that justice one day will be done'. Perhaps this plea had now been answered.

It was never established beyond doubt whether Carter had intended to also kill his son or merely to add a sickening gravitas to the faked robbery and assault scenario. Whilst six-year-old Alun lay unconscious in hospital he remained a ticking time-bomb for his father who must have prayed for his demise, all the while keeping a perverse vigil at his son's bedside. On his discharge some three weeks after gaining consciousness a frail and bewildered Alun would be entrusted to the care of his paternal grandparents in Cowbridge. The thankless task of explaining both his mother's grisly demise and his father's imprisonment would lie ahead.

Chapter 13

Found Dead in St Mary's Graveyard: Margaret Sennett Bute Street 1969

Margaret Winifred Sennett would have been twenty-four years old in March 1969 had her life not been so cruelly ended on the cold Saturday night of 5 January. Originally from Adamsdown, she was now living in a flat in Compton Street in Grangetown. A somewhat serious girl, her old friends recalled her as a staunch Catholic during her time as a pupil at Lady Mary's School in Cyncoed. Unmarried, she now had a two-month-old son. Paul Anthony was however not her first-born child. Poor Margaret. What a waste. The blow of the premature death of her first child two years earlier aged just a few months had been a devastating blow to the young woman. She had retreated in to her grief and withdrawn from the normality of daily life. There was neither time nor inclination to chat with neighbours and friends. Then, with the birth of the second child, came a new incentive to reconnect with those around her so proud was she of the little boy. 'She was full of talk and starting to make new friends' said the proprietor of her corner shop. With a new confidence and a need to communicate again she was soon returning to the old drinking haunts vacated during her pregnancy.

Prior to being heavily pregnant with Paul, Margaret had worked as a packer in a Docks' factory. Now unemployed, she had drifted far too easily from lonely single mother bereft of a steady wage to part-time prostitute. The selling of her body was no vocation but a lesson in the harsh reality that poverty teaches people. It was the means to an end to feed and clothe both her and the baby. Not unattractive and with a cheerful disposition she would find it relatively easy money and her paying admirers many. A network of friends would care for her child while she escaped the confines of her dingy flat to work the bustling public houses along the Bute Street and Custom House Street strip. Her method of work was a low rent honeytrap. She did not walk the dockland streets but chose to sit alone in local pubs nursing a solitary drink until a gentleman pulled up a chair to join her keen to strike up a conversation and more. Maybe unpopular among the public houses' female clientele, both regular and professional, bar staff would note that lady friends were on the whole absent but this was certainly compensated by a steady flow of male attention.

Her pleasures were modest and few with a regular Sunday night seat at a Canton Bingo Hall her weekly treat. It would be her inexplicable non appearance to play there on the night of 6 January that first alerted her friends as to something being

At the time of Margaret's Sennett's death North Church Street in the shadow of St Mary's was still populated in the wake of mass demolition of the old Butetown. The author

amiss. Subsequent phone calls would glean that she had not indeed returned home the night before.

With the report of the woman's disappearance reaching the attention of the local constabulary the latter half of the Sunday would prompt a conspicuous uniformed police presence in Butetown. All too aware of the precarious nature of a life like Margaret Sennett's, their search was for anyone or anything that could divulge her whereabouts either dead or alive. At 11.15 that night PC Ronald Naish made the discovery that they had feared. Here was Margaret; cold, dead and partially naked slumped in the close confines of the disused boiler house in the rear grounds of the Church of St Mary the Virgin situated at the 'town end' of Bute Street. Under the leaves and wooden debris that acted as her shroud, torchlight exposed livid burn marks and scarring to her eyes, face and upper torso. It was deduced that she had lain there for some twenty-four hours having been dragged a short distance to the dirty outhouse post-mortem.

So that was it. Young Margaret was dead and the police were geared up for this eventuality. Within minutes a massive murder hunt was launched in earnest with three teams of detectives under the direction of Detective Chief Superintendent David Morris. The Cardiff force had been bitterly stung earlier in the decade with the killing of a prostitute and they were not about to repeat their failings. Back in November 1963 the body of twenty-year-old Patricia Simpson was discovered at the bottom of a 230ft deep disused iron-ore shaft in Pentyrch. She had been strangled. Originally from Lancashire, she had made her home in Cardiff's Adamsdown frequently travelling to nearby Butetown to ply her trade. The parallels with the life and death of Margaret Sennett were something that local police were only too aware. Despite an investigation lasting well into the summer of 1964 and the aid of Scotland Yard specialists the Cardiff police were ultimately left with nothing to point to Simpson's killer and the case was ruefully and humiliatingly shelved unsolved.

Margaret's indecent resting place, the rear of St Mary's resembled a bombsite but closer inspection would reveal that it was the rubble of Butetown houses only recently demolished as

The rear of St. Mary's seen today. Margaret's Sennett's lifeless body was secreted in a small outhouse since demolished. It was originally located to the left of the arched church entrance (now closed) at the centre of picture. The author

Now a car park, the area on the North Church Street side of St. Mary's was in 1969 a grassed area secluded by a row of mature trees. The author

part of the city's controversial regeneration of the dockland area. Amid the detritus of people's lives lay the old mattresses, wardrobes, bicycles and toys abandoned by their former owners when vacating their homes. The stone and brick awaiting clearance from here and simultaneously in Lower Splott lay as a suitable epitaph for Cardiff communities now long gone. The ugly, functional blocks of the new Loudon Square were yet to come. In the gaze of the church's twin towers this some-how godforsaken patch played host to children's games by day and the illicit activities of adults by night; a secluded overspill from the trade on the main drag of Bute Street.

It was not the first time that the solid Victorian pile of St Mary the Virgin had been linked with murder – albeit in fiction. It is doubtful though that many outside the local area would recall it. In the British film thriller *Tiger Bay* set in Cardiff and released in 1960 the church was the place where a young chorister Gillie Evans played by Hayley Mills chose to hide the gun that she had found stashed in her lodging house. The weapon had previously been used to deadly effect on the

The impressive frontage of the Church of St Mary the Virgin, long a landmark in the ever changing face of Butetown. The author

unfaithful girlfriend of a Polish seaman. In the film, the killer is portrayed as an intrinsically good man who had snapped during a moment of extreme provocation. His later rescuing of Mills, as his young companion, from drowning thus exposing himself to capture and arrest comes as a fitting act of atonement at the film's denouement. There would be no such generosity of spirit or redemption in the squalid shadow of St Mary's in 1969.

Forensic reports on the body of Margaret Sennett were to be carried out at the Cardiff Royal Infirmary by Professor Bernard Knight. He officially recorded death by asphyxia following manual strangulation. The deep wealds on her body had been caused by an unsuccessful attempt at burning her clothing, the nylon composition of her outfit and the dampness of the surroundings had put paid to this plan. Despite this partial destruction of the garments it was clearly apparent that some items of her clothing were missing.

With families still living in North Church Street mere yards away from the murder scene initial enquiries in the local area were positive. Investigators were soon to piece together an informed picture of the woman's last known movements on Saturday night. Perhaps they were even *too* positive; such were the number of people who knew Margaret and had seen or spoken to her during the final night of her life that progress could only be made via a series of identity parades and a laborious process of elimination. Keen officers would notice the similarity between the victim's death and that of a similar case in Hartlepool, County Durham earlier in the month. Shipping records were meticulously examined to ascertain whether any vessel from that port had been berthed in Cardiff over that weekend but there were none. With this information the theory of an errant seaman was officially brushed aside.

That Saturday had seen a massive influx of people heading for Ninian Park to watch Cardiff City play Arsenal in the third round of the FA Cup. Many of those 55,000 fans who had witnessed a draw stayed on in town after the game to eat, drink and make merry. That evening, the ever lively bars of Butetown would have their regular weekend clientele quadrupled by the hoards of thirsty football fans. Did any of those out-of-towners make the acquaintance of poor Margaret that night?

Manhunt

The nightmare scenario for police could not simply be discarded. If their initial hunch *was* incorrect and the killer was not a local man then he could easily be one of the nameless tens of thousands who had descended on the city that day for the cup game at Ninian Park. If so, it was quite feasible that the killer may now be safely ensconced in any part of the UK let alone the respective teams' heartlands of South Wales and North London. And, with his fleeing, so would the trail to his identity have turned icy cold.

With subsequent leads and enquiries in the South Wales valleys going nowhere the Cardiff constabulary would hold their nerve and resolutely set their sights on the killer being a Cardiff man to the exclusion of all others. The initial list of those of interest to the investigation was supplied by a Vice Squad au fait with the habitual users of local prostitutes. That list was depressingly long. The main hurdle for investigators was to convince those acquainted with Sennett to make themselves known to the police, their particular association with the deceased most likely unknown to wives, girlfriends and children. The promise of anonymity if innocent helped to loosen many a reticent tongue. It would soon become a numbers game. That week officers working in day and night shifts would interview 400 men and take over 150 statements. At one point forty-five detectives were simultaneously putting in gruelling individual sixteen hour stints. In the final round-up just twenty names would remain as priority for investigators and a police spokesman would cryptically inform the public that five unspecified Cardiff locations, key to their enquiries, were subject to round the clock surveillance should their man appear.

The bulk of the meticulously gathered information resolutely pointed to their man being a 'casual' acquaintance of Margaret with local intelligence further indicating that he was employed as a labourer. Working on this assumption a call was put out to local doctor's surgeries, hospitals and building site foremen to be on the alert for any man bearing tell tale facial injuries that may have resulted from the victim's spirited struggle. By way of sheer determination by 9 January detectives had narrowed their search to just one man.

It was obvious that detectives believed that there was something to be gleaned from close observance of mourners at Margaret's funeral at Ely's Western Cemetery. Her service had fittingly been held at St Mary the Virgin the very place where she had met her brutal demise. Plain clothes men mingled with the crowds of onlookers as her coffin passed strewn with red and white carnations. Perhaps they had hoped that it was just possible, however unlikely that a pang of guilt or some deep remorse may cajole a one time friend turned killer into the open. The investigators would have no such luck.

There would be a breakthrough. A fellow prostitute and friend of the victim came forward to say that she had spoken to Margaret on Bute Street quite likely less than thirty minutes before her death. Most important of all she could give a detailed description of the tragic woman's companion:

I came across the couple on Bute Street at about 11 p.m. When I was about four foot from them I recognised Margaret and as I had not seen her for three weeks I asked her how she was. She told me she was all right and told me that she would be at the bingo on Sunday. As I turned to go to my mother's house down the docks I saw her walk with the man down North Church Street and they disappeared along the railings in the dark towards the church.

So wary were the police as to the safety of their witness that her identity was shielded throughout and she was instructed to stay away from Butetown and the Docks lest a savage retribution should be metered upon her. Her first hand account of the last sighting of Margaret and the man suspected of brutal murder was of the utmost importance to his apprehension and conviction. For reasons never made clear detectives were anxious to distribute photo-fit pictures of their prime suspect among the drinkers in Butetown while at the same time refusing to put details of the man's likeness in the wider public domain via the *South Wales Echo*. The reason given for this was that the public may be 'confused' by the suspect's description. 'Confused' is a strange word here. Police were certain as to the accuracy of their informant's account and as such the resultant photographic likeness. What separated a member of the public being shown a photo in a pub and someone viewing the same picture in a newspaper? If they feared that their man would bolt if his face was made public in the press they severely under-estimated the power of the local grapevine to alert him as to the closing of the net. The police were fortunate; their man was going nowhere. A combination of sheer determination and subsequently highly commended detective work would lead the police to finally make an arrest on 13 January 1969.

The trial

Royston Churchill Slater was twenty-eight years old and employed as a labourer. Like many a male war baby he had been saddled with the name of the country's almost mythic wartime Prime Minister but none of the heroic magic that went with such a bestowal had rubbed off upon the boy. He had endured a troubled childhood and, from the age of twenty had appeared in court on numerous occasions, charged with theft, breaking and entering, 'going equipped', vehicle theft and assault. More disturbingly, Slater was no 'ordinary' criminal. In 1967 he had been detained in hospital under the Mental Health Act after being caught breaking in to a shop. He managed to abscond seven times from the hospital in Bristol before his eventual discharge in August of that year. Within twelve months of his release he had been charged with a violent assault on his mother-in-law. Like Margaret, he too had a young child of a near identical age to that of hers who lived with him and his wife in Habershon Street in Splott.

Having been held in custody by order of John Rutter the city Stipendiary Magistrate, Slater's short trial would conclude on 17 January at the Glamorgan Assizes in Cardiff. The prosecution, under the direction of Phillip Wren QC, contended that Slater had become a client of Sennett some time around 10.30pm and before sexual intercourse had taken place a violent argument had ensued probably over the sum of money involved. Sennett's assailant consequently rendered her semiconscious with a brutal series of punches to the face before killing her by strangulation. Then, undoubtedly motivated by avarice rather than the desire for some sort of sick trophy Slater proceeded to remove items of clothing and jewellery from Sennett's body and handbag. His initial attempts to set fire to her body rendered futile by the cold damp weather conditions, within an hour of her death, Slater had returned to his family home in Splott.

It would be Margaret Sennett's stolen possessions that would damn him. Their ownership by the dead woman was incontrovertible. Less than two hours after Margaret's death Slater's unwitting wife was trying on clothes, a ring and a wristwatch so recently stripped from her corpse. In an act of desperate bravado Slater would claim that these tawdry gifts to his spouse had been bought in Gloucester and challenged detectives to prove otherwise. They could easily do so. He had prepared no such story to account for his maroon corduroy jacket worn on the night of Sennett's murder being flecked with her blood.

He claimed that on the night of the 4th he had been drinking in the *Pierhead Hotel* only to leave at around 10.15pm and had proceeded alone along Bute Street towards the bus station. From there he caught the bus to Splott arriving home at around 11pm. Needless to say, he had no one to corroborate this semi-bogus journey.

If anything, Slater's 'mistake' was to kill a woman so well known, on the very patch where she worked *and* within minutes of being sighted in her company. With a volatile temper and a less than firm grip on reality his actions were predominantly beyond his control. An examination of the accused undertaken by Dr Dennis Powell of Cardiff Prison decreed that Morris in his opinion was 'mentally abnormal and his abnormality was sufficient to impair his responsibility'. With this assessment, John Blackburn Gittings acting for the accused entered a plea of 'not guilty' to the charge of murder but guilty of the lesser charge of manslaughter. This compromise was regarded as the only way to proceed and as such was agreed to by prosecution council and presiding judge, Mr Justice McKenna alike. It was ruled that the severity and dangerous nature of Slater's mental disorder would discount a prison term. Imposing a restriction order under Section 65 of the Mental Health Act 'necessary for the protection of the public', Slater would be allocated a place at the notorious Rampton Hospital for 'special treatment', his incarceration period indefinite.

What does it leave us? Two children growing up confused and bewildered. Devoid of a mother. Devoid of a father. Might they say: 'My mother was a prostitute out on the streets to earn enough to buy me food and clothes?' or 'My father was insane and cruelly robbed and murdered a young woman in a spiteful rage?' As I write this I have no idea if either child is still alive. If indeed they are then they would have not yet reached their fortieth birthday. Your author is of a similar age. Sitting here at a café table in a Cardiff suburb, I wonder if have they passed me in the street, stood next to me in a supermarket queue – perhaps even collected their own children from my son's school playground? And I wonder too what damage the weight of their corrosive memories and regret might be – and it makes me shudder.

Chapter 14

The Shocking Electrocution of Glenys Darling Llandaff 1977

I must at this time make no comment on a sad event in the parish during the past month which shocked and saddened us. Please remember Barry Darling in your prayers. I am grateful to all those who so speedily offered practical help in the care of Barry's children and especially to Mr and Mrs Ron Roberts with whom Shareena and Darren stayed until they were able to go to their own family.

The sincerity of these words penned by Alun Davis, the Dean of Llandaff Cathedral, as part of his published monthly missive is beyond doubt. Sadly though, his turn of phrase is open to question and perhaps even touched with grimly inappropriate and unintended irony. The 'event' to which the Dean somewhat cautiously and somewhat obliquely referred to as 'shocking' was in fact a shock of the electric kind – the horrific electrocution of Glenys Darling, the wife of one of his very own staff.

Thirty-three-year-old James Barry Darling had spent the majority of his life in Yorkshire. His years there had been on the whole unremarkable. Only his stint as a drummer in a local pop band had enlivened a *curriculum vitae* of labouring and window cleaning. It also brought in extra income too – much needed by his wife and young children, Shareena and Darren. Their friends and neighbours had been genuinely surprised when the marriage turned sour resulting in a separation that left Barry Darling looking after his two children alone. The marital disruption and added responsibility might have broken a lesser man but Darling had become a committed Christian and he turned to his faith to help him pull through. Even at the time some of his more cynical fellow parishioners doubted the expediency of his newly cultivated religious zeal. Whatever the case, could his faith not only bolster him but be the path to a newer, better life?

Darling became consumed by the notion of moving away and starting life afresh. He began to scan the situations vacant columns of the ecclesiastic journals. Possibly reaching beyond his calling he had once tried and failed to train for the priesthood in the Church of England. Even as a member of the local Parochial Church Council it was perhaps time to scale down his ambitions. In early 1977 he saw his opportunity and snatched at it. He applied for the post of Assistant Verger at Llandaff Cathedral in Cardiff: a spectacular building in picturesque surroundings to say nothing of its role as one of the most important centres of faith in the Principality. A dream come true.

His application had been favourably received by the selection board. After all, it had come with a personal recommendation from the Bishop of Pontefract no less that vouched for Darling as a *committed Christian and likeable young man*. But there was an important and potentially devastating caveat to the job offer. His potential employers would look more favourably on a married man. Unwelcome news to a divorcee with two children.

In an attempt that must have seemed futile from the outset Darling immediately set about brokering a reconciliation with his ex-wife. This desperate plan came to nothing and forced Darling to think again. He needed a 'Plan B' and he needed it quickly. He found it in the shape of a pretty twenty-six-year-old fellow chorister named Glenys. We shall never know how much genuine affection (if any at all) Darling felt for this ill-fated woman – suffice it to say that he successfully wooed and wed her after a whirlwind romance lasting weeks rather than months. After just two days of marriage, in February 1977, the couple and his two children upped sticks from their native Yorkshire and moved into their new home in Cardiff. Appearing like every 'young married couple' cliché in the book their apparent happiness would be short-lived and their stay brutally truncated.

The close-knit, conservative community in and around the cathedral soon became aware that it was far from marital bliss in the Darling household. Ensconced in the charming Well Cottage sited on the Village Close, Barry Darling was viewed as an affable hardworking young man but his wife however was judged to be withdrawn and unhappy with her lot. The sudden wrench away from family and friends in Yorkshire and the apparently difficult relationship with her husband's children were beginning to take their toll. Her life was rapidly disintegrating into one of self-doubt and regret.

Matters would come to a horrific climax on the evening of 17 October 1977. Before the night was out Glenys Darling was no more. She would die in agony – the victim of a massive electric shock whilst sitting in the bath. A gruesome death punctuated by screams, convulsions and a mass of sparks. An electric fan-heater was found submerged in the water. The post-mortem carried out the following morning doubled the tragedy. She had been three months pregnant. Described by observers as strangely 'cool and composed', Barry Darling was escorted from the scene by police as the ambulance arrived. With the death treated as suspicious Darling began to be questioned as the only person capable of providing anything tangible to explain the events leading up to his wife's demise.

From the outset Darling's manner troubled the South Wales Constabulary detectives assigned to the case. Could a husband claiming to be so distraught by his wife's death be sat so calmly, glass of sherry in hand, awaiting an ambulance? Why did he not instinctively pull the heater's plug from the socket when entering the bathroom? She was dead – wasn't she? Why go all the way downstairs to turn the power off at the mains? He had not even done *this* until after he called for an ambulance.

Darling was to fare very badly under 'persistent and lively' questioning. It appeared that thinking on his feet was certainly not his forte and his version of that night's events underwent revision and correction the more he spoke. At first he claimed that he was outside in the garden at the crucial moment alerted to his wife's distress only by a blood curdling scream emanating from the cottage's bathroom. A horrible accident unseen by the suspect must have occurred.

Although the police dutifully paid lip service to pursuing other lines of enquiry the team, under the direction of Detective Chief Inspector Raymond Hill, knew instinctively that Darling had not only witnessed his wife's death but was also responsible for it. The notion of accidental death or even manslaughter was far removed from the minds of the South Wales Constabulary. They observed their prime suspect as cold and calculating but his attempts to explain his involvement or lack of it were naively flawed. The investigating officers truly believed that the pressure of intense questioning would coax out the truth and with this agenda they set about their task. The police persistently broached the subject of Darling's faith and Christian duty to tell the truth at any cost. They believed that this would be Darling's achilles heel and their persistence was to soon pay dividends.

Forensic testing on the electric heater rubber stamped the foregone conclusion that Mrs Darling's death had been caused by a massive electric shock facilitated by the appliance being submerged in her bath water. Moreover, and crucial to the enquiry, the testing also established the fact that any inherent fault in the appliance was not down to wear and tear. The all important earth terminals in the plug had been tampered with and left lethally disconnected. With this information and another round of intense questioning Darling 'confessed'. He had witnessed Glenys' death. So frustrated had he been with his wife's habit of taking the electric heater into the chilly bathroom that he had decided that he wanted to frighten her out of her complacency. Going to help her rinse her hair in the bath as was his routine he had held the heater up over the bath water and berated her as to its potential danger. In one horrific moment, the heater had accidentally slipped from his hand into the water. Darling even willingly wrote out his own 'confession' – a very rare occurrence. The longer that he elaborated the more convoluted and unbelievable his account became. Perhaps sensing his interrogators' incredulity, Darling embarked on his third and final version of events leading up to his wife's death. The police finally had what they had been working towards. Darling now admitted that in one rash moment he had purposely let the heater slip into the bath. As he put it he wanted 'to teach her a lesson' – to give her a jolt; something to think about. 'An immediate shock,' he said. To frighten but not to kill. 'I really did not mean to harm my wife. I really did love her.' On 19 October 1977, just forty-eight hours after his wife's death, James Barry Darling was formally charged with her murder.

Throughout the week-long trial at Cardiff Crown Court Darling resolutely denied malice aforethought and continued to portray himself as a grieving husband beset by tragedy. He would accept the charge of manslaughter by default. Few present in the courtroom felt that his defence – David Williams QC – put up anything more than an arbitrary rebuttal of the charge of premeditated murder though in balance, with the weight of evidence to the contrary, he could sustain little else. For the prosecution, Aubrey Myerson certainly had more to work with, dismissing Darling's testimony in the witness box as 'a tissue of lies'. The most damning evidence rested on the accused's professed ignorance of all electrical matters. Could it be that a thirty-three-year-old man even be incapable of wiring a domestic plug? Possibly yes, but extremely unlikely. Darling had been known to carry out minor electrical repairs around his home so his protestations of ignorance were dubious in the extreme. The final blow was to come from a most unexpected source. The very day of his wife's death Darling had visited his local public library and borrowed a volume on household electrics and fitted a new plug to the heater. The book contained a chapter entitled 'Power points and earthing'. With the revelation of this bibliographic aid to murder the prosecution rested its case.

Justice Tasker Watkins presiding over the case concluded his closing address to the jury thus:

Manslaughter it has been said is a serious crime. But the fact that it is a serious crime which he clearly admits that he is guilty of must not in anyway influence you in deciding whether he is guilty of the more serious crime of murder. A young woman's life has been abruptly ended in a criminal way. What precisely that crime is, from the evidence presented, you tell me.

And tell him they did. The trial reached its conclusion on 21 March 1978. After two hours the jury comprising of seven men and two women reached a verdict. They were unanimous. Darling was guilty of murder as charged. As the judge sentenced him to life imprisonment Darling remained motionless and held his silence in the dock. Turning to Darling, Justice Tasker Watkins said:

> *Every now and again the judge has the misfortune to look upon a cold-blooded killer. I have that misfortune now.*

Postscript
It seems almost obligatory that a story as tragic as this should have an equally grim postscript. On 7 August 1998 holiday-makers spotted a body floating in the Calder & Hebble Canal at Copley, near Halifax. When eventually identified, the body was found to be that of fifty-six-year-old James Barry Darling. Released from prison eight years earlier, he had suffered from bouts of depression and had twice attempted to take his own life. He had found work again as a verger on release. The vicar at Leeds Parish Church had only become aware of Darling's death when contacting probation officers as to his non appearance for work. The Reverend Cornwell commented: 'He was on licence for the rest of his life but I was told that there was some possibility of his licence being revoked. I don't know why.'

Could it have been the fear of a return to incarceration that lured non-swimmer Darling into the water to terminate his life or maybe something more prosaic? Is it too trite to think that memories of his crime twenty years earlier had become so engulfing, so overwhelming that suicide could be his only release? The Assistant Coroner, Mark Hinchcliffe certainly believed so. At Darling's inquest, with West Yorkshire Police finding no suspicious circumstances, he concluded that Darling has taken his own life because of 'all consuming misery'.

Then, as now, one can only speculate as to Darling's motives for the killing of his wife. A violent act that would make some twisted sense if carried out during an insane rage is rendered incomprehensible by the evidence of planning and deceit. With a trail of actions that simply cry out 'murder' could Darling ever have thought for even one moment that he might quite literally 'get away' with it? This would surely strain the limits of anyone's credulity and prove to be a monumental gamble. Was his wife's pregnant state influential on his grotesque scheme or merely a tragic adjunct? There seems so little that could be gained by his wife's death – financial or otherwise – that might precipitate such a callous act. One thing *is* for sure; Barry Darling as good as killed himself that night he slew his wife. Like Glenys in 1977, his too would be a watery grave. But not for him a quick exit from this mortal coil. Twenty wretched years of regret – a fitting postponement to the eventual murder of himself and his guilty memories.

Chapter 15

The Unsolved Killing of Jack Armstrong Cardiff 1979

The killing

With 'Williams' sitting in the back seat of the cab one can only assume that Jack Armstrong had little warning before receiving the first of a series of sickening blows to the head. Hopefully the first rendered him mercifully unconscious. The car was most likely to have been stationary at the time of the assault – not even a psychopath such as his assailant would risk his *own* life by battering someone in control of a moving vehicle. By the nature and positioning of the bloodstains in the car's interior the police would deduce that the bulk of the vicious attack took place outside the vehicle – possible even that all of the deadly

Cowbridge Common (aka Stalling Down) Jack Armstrong was slain and his body dumped in broad daylight at this desolate spot. The author

strikes were delivered in the open air. Did family man Jack beg for his life kneeling on the damp scrubland of the common? Only one man alive knows. Dead or dying, Jack Armstrong's elderly body was dragged away from sight of the road and half secreted in undergrowth. A shabby resting place for this popular, good natured gentleman.

Finding the car

At 4.45 in the afternoon, the car – a 1975 metallic bronze Colt Sigma saloon – was eventually located. It lay abandoned in the cul-de-sac that is Treoes Lane – a short obscure road on the fringe of a Bridgend Industrial estate. Doors open and bloodstained, its appearance betrayed signs of a violent struggle. Ominously its owner, fifty-eight-year-old taxi cab driver Jack Armstrong was nowhere to be seen. Evidence at the site indicated that at the very least the missing man had sustained serious injuries. Within the hour the setting up of an incident room in Bridgend under the command of the head of South Wales CID

Treoes Lane which once linked the village of Coychurch with that of Treoes seen from the Treoes side. It was here in what was by then a secluded cul-de-sac that Armstrong's cab was abandoned. The author

Detective Chief Superintendent Viv Brook would herald a full-scale murder hunt. For the first time in his career he would order the setting up of a second room, in Cardiff, to handle investigations relating to the initial stage of the taxi cab's fateful journey. With the remote possibility that Armstrong may still be lying somewhere clinging on to life, an immediate and massive search was launched co-opting local farmers and the Army to assist the 100 or so police officers determinedly scouring the vast rural area between Bridgend and Cardiff bordering the A48 dual carriageway. Simultaneously, detectives would engage in a methodical trawl for witnesses concentrating on the Cardiff location of the cab's last known pick-up and its final dumping on the eastern outskirts of Bridgend. Bizarrely, police were to later discover Jack Armstrong's driving licence and personal documents in a hedge in Treoes Lane, wrapped in a bloody rag. From their positioning it was obvious that they had been deliberately hidden there. One can only guess at the killer's logic for this action. The only plausible explanation was that 'Williams' had sought to impede identification of his victim, an absolutely futile attempt in the light of the taxi cab's registration number and markings. Whatever his reasoning, the luck of the devil was with 'Williams'. Forensic tests on the bloodstained belongings produced nothing of merit.

Leading pathologist Professor Bernard Knight would later at the inquest attribute cause of death to extensive skull fractures and damage to the brain. The senseless brutality of the slaying and its subsequent pitiful financial haul for the killer was quite incomprehensible. The police declared that the motive for the assault was robbery – there was little else to say. Could the killer really have plotted and manoeuvred his victim to make off with a sum reckoned to be between just twelve and twenty pounds? After smashing the facia of the dashboard he had also tried and failed to steal the car's radio. Certainly not a king's ransom even thirty years ago. Such cruelty, such barbarity – *for that*? 'Williams' would have had no way of knowing how much Jack Armstrong would be carrying in his cab and indeed whether he was starting or nearing the end of a lucrative shift. There surely must have been a less risky way of dishonestly obtaining a relatively small amount of cash without initiating this horror.

Those attempting to 'get into' the mind set of a killer have an onerous task. It's chilling to muse on whether 'Williams' really just wanted to kill from the outset. No other motivation; the driver's takings merely beer money.

The facts

With a chain of events uncertain and a bloody conclusion seemingly flying in the face of logic it is so tempting to project assumptions and dress them as fact. What is it that we actually *know*? An accurate chronology of that fateful day is scant: Friday 5 October 1979. At around half past one in the afternoon father of five, taxi-driver John (known as 'Jack') Armstrong collected a fare from outside the *Fairwater Hotel*, a popular public house in a western suburb of Cardiff. The customer had phoned the office of Castle Cabs and booked the car under the name of Williams. At around 1.35pm Armstrong radioed his controller to acknowledge picking up the man. These were to be his last known words as approximately a half hour later he was to be horrifically bludgeoned to death.

The car park of the Fairwater Hotel. It was here that Jack Armstrong was to collect his final fare. The author

Search for the body

Investigators discounted the possibility that Armstrong had been in the cab when it arrived at Treoes Lane. They were correct to do so. With grim inevitability Jack Armstrong's battered corpse was stumbled across partially interred in dense undergrowth and bracken in a spot almost invisible from the nearby road. This was Monday 8 October – some three days after the discovery of his car. The location was the lonely Stalling Down (sometimes known as Cowbridge Common) on the eastern edge of the market town of Cowbridge, some sixteen or so miles west along the A48 from Cardiff and eleven miles away from the discovery of the car.

From the outset the police had strongly suspected that the weapon that had smashed the driver's skull like an egg shell was a heavy object with a circular metal end. It was most likely

The Coychurch 'end' of Treoes Lane. It was deduced that Armstrong's killer made good his escape via this obscure route thus strongly indicating a man in possession of a distinct degree of local knowledge. The author

a form of 'lump hammer' – a common professional builder's tool. This theory was substantiated by the account of a man unsuccessfully touting for work on the day of the slaying at a building site close to the *Fairwater Hotel*. Such was the match between the detailed description of the jobseeker and a man observed jumping into Armstrong's cab in the pub car park carrying what could have easily been a haversack full of tools, that investigators were to stake all on that they were one and the same. What was to baffle detectives throughout the murder hunt was the whereabouts of their man 'Williams' in the hours between visiting the building site and entering Armstrong's cab – some three hours. Despite exhaustive inquiries taking in local pubs, clubs, cafes and other building sites the issue of these 'missing' hours would never be resolved.

South Wales Police wasted little time in releasing a photo-fit picture of their prime suspect to the local press. The man believed to be 'Williams' was described as being around thirty years old, 6 feet tall and of a slim build. He sported collar-length brown hair and appeared 'well groomed'. One thing was certain. With his smart, casual clothes he had definitely not just stepped off a site – this was not labouring attire. Astonishingly, a female taxi-driver would attest to driving the man in the photo-fit twice to the Stalling Down murder site in recent weeks. Could his connection to the area be the key to the identity of the so called 'cool, calculating killer?' The picture, considered by all to be a remarkable likeness, soon had its desired effect. A myriad of credible sightings of both man and car were reported by the public. A palpably excited investigation team could now pinpoint the killer's movements both before and immediately after the murder: 'I think we can almost plot him along every inch of the route' reported a buoyant Viv Brook. This information would in turn inform the route of a reconstruction of the journey in which two officers took on the morbid duty of driving Armstrong's car from Cardiff theatrically bundling out a dummy on their arrival at Stalling Down. A team of detectives were on hand to speak to potential witnesses their memories jogged by the recreation. As hoped, the recollections flooded in and the police anticipated a breakthrough. They waited for the one significant witness who could lay this case wide open. So they waited.

The first person that detectives made public that they were seeking to eliminate from their enquiries was a motorist that had been parked in Treoes Lane at exactly the same time that the taxi cab was dumped there. A witness driving past described a man asleep at the wheel of a 'modern' car. The 'sleeping man' came forward. A commercial traveller, he had merely been slumped in his seat reading his company notes. Eliminated from the inquiry, he was said to have supplied the team with excellent information – the details never disclosed by a tight-lipped police force. This would mark a high point of expectation but the steady flow of intelligence in regard to the murder would soon stagnate.

The suspects
The onset of winter 1979, and now so many suspects to muddy the waters. The hitcher, the sleeper, the drunks, the French girl's beau – butcher, baker, candlestick maker? With so many seemingly positive sightings of their prime suspect, each witness' recollection of 'Williams' dress and physical features so remarkably similar, the police's confidence in an immanent arrest had been understandably high. All over by Christmas – surely? How cruel fate can be when it robs you of your certainties.

The investigation would soon get tangled in a morass of false leads and false hope. With twisted logic the more vigorously they pursued their man the more contradictory and confused their information would become. The shreds of evidence pointing to the identity of the killer that recently seemed so tantalizingly close were evaporating before their very eyes. Who are you Williams? Where are you now? The detectives' fingers slowly slipping away from the coat tails of this spectre along the highway.

On the afternoon of the murder one man witnesses Jack Armstrong's Castle Cabs car speeding dangerously around the Waterston Industrial Estate, only to suddenly brake and swerve into Treoes Lane – its final dumping ground. Remarkably, this eyewitness swears that he spots its driver 'Williams' *again* a week later; this time as a passenger getting into a taxi on the same estate outside the premises of Groom & Llewellyn. By coincidence this second sighting of the suspect would take place on the same afternoon as the painstaking police reconstruction of the murder route. The inertia and silence that would dog the whole inquiry would once again become apparent. By the time police establish the name of the taxi firm in question records of that day's fares had been 'inadvertently destroyed' and, true to form, the police's desperate appeal for the driver to come forward proves fruitless. This would set an ominous precedent.

During this crucial week another character would also be added to the roster of those persons 'actively sought'. Detectives made public that they were seeking the identity of a hitch-hiker who had been picked up in Cowbridge. The hitcher had explained that he was trying to get to Llantwit Major having left his vehicle overnight in Cardiff. The driver of the car became suspicious when the man subsequently contradicted himself by asking to be dropped off at Llanmaes claiming that his car was actually parked near the village of Boverton. This, along with the hitcher's attire being not too dissimilar to accounts of 'Williams' clothing would create a heady brew in this first frantic week of the murder hunt. Despite an appeal in the press the man was never traced.

For reasons never made abundantly clear attention soon turned to two local men who had shared a taxi ride together a week after the killing. Their journey originated close to the

large L'Oreal factory where they were picked up along the road that links Talbot Green to Llanharan. Their destination was Llanbradach near the town of Caerphilly. On this occasion the men were successfully traced via the records of the Porth based taxi hire firm. With neither

The photofit picture of a man sought by the South Wales police in connection with the murder of Jack Armstrong. Released to the press on 16 October 1979 – to the bitter regret of the detectives it did little to progress the investigation.
South Wales Police

judged to have any connection with the killing as swiftly as they had drifted on to enquiry's radar screen so did they drift away.

The family

Jack Armstrong's family could neither forgive nor forget. His cruel death had left them devastated. The murder had taken place just a week before what would have been his ninth wedding anniversary. His grieving widow Evelyn in her Llanederyn home finally found composure to release a statement to the press. In it she tearfully said:

> *It's been almost four weeks now and I feel that if we can do anything to help it is time for us to speak out. It's obvious that someone knows something about this man. Will they please come forward to help us? What this man had done nothing can put right. But we want him caught for the safety of other people, especially taxi-drivers.*

The tragic loss would cut deep into the lives of his children too. One of the victim's sons, David, then aged nineteen found it impossible to proceed with arrangements for his wedding that Christmas choosing to postpone it out of respect for his father. Jack Armstrong had indeed been much loved. Even some of his regular female customers found it difficult to speak of him without breaking down in tears.

Desperation – 'French Connection'

November 1979. A new month and a tantalising new direction for a murder inquiry rapidly turning stale. Admitting concern that results of the local investigation were at the very least disappointing, South Wales CID declared their intention to trace and question some French girls who had been camping in the Cowbridge area during the August and September. With some of their names already known, police in Brittany were handed the task of finding the women. Police in South Wales were anxious to identify a man whom it was thought had visited the French girls at their campsite. Crucially he had twice taken a taxi journey to Stalling Down in the week prior to Jack Armstrong's murder. Brashly dubbed 'The French connection' by the local press, this avenue of enquiry was to eventually prove a red herring. In the public perception this was perhaps the tipping point at which the dynamism and impetus of the initial murder hunt would now look like a scramble with a faint whiff of desperation. Had after only a month the case gone completely cold? Hindsight is a wonderful thing.

'Local man' – Brynna?

The police were to *constantly* distil and refine the sightings and snippets of information in regard to 'Williams' to the point at which they were now convinced that their killer was indeed a local man with a hard connection to the Bridgend closing area of the 'murder route' as opposed to its Cardiff start. 'Williams' was in effect a commuter travelling daily to Cardiff either to work or search for work. They were to go further still and make it public that they were now concentrating on the village of Brynna on the outskirts of Bridgend as the killer's abode. Whatever intelligence directed them to this particular location was kept tightly close to their chest. They were surely not in a position to make a pronouncement such as this based on mere supposition. Investigators believed that 'Williams' had been more than familiar with both the murder site and the car's dumping ground. Again, their reasoning was never made absolutely explicit. Treoes Lane had once been a through road, the construction of a stretch of the M4 motorway putting paid to that some years before. It was reckoned that 'Williams' knew it of old as the short-cut to Coychurch that it once was and chose it as his dumping ground. Did it provide an easy exit for him? Easy access to public transport?

The murder investigation was not without dark humour. An eyewitness claimed to have seen 'Williams' board the 2.33pm Bridgend to Pontypridd bus on the afternoon of the killing. Getting on at Coychurch he was to alight before it had reached Tonteg. The witness saw the man in conversation with a pair of drunks on the bus. The police issued an appeal to trace the 'whisky drinking men' in the local press. When eventually found the men could not even recall being on the bus let alone identify any fellow passengers.

Aftermath

Years later, freed of professional restraint by his retirement, Brook would openly lay part of the blame for the police's failure with the 'complete lack of help' from fellow taxi-drivers. Harsh words and of course subjective. After all, these were the men who had raised both money for the widow and part of the substantial reward for the killer's apprehension. Is it sadly true that the fear of some drivers being caught 'moonlighting' deterred them from coming forward? Police had given definite reassurances to the contrary to allay their fears during the initial investigation. Through the autumn and winter of 1979 taxi firm boss Arnold Dickson had implored his employees to assist the investigating officers with any scrap of information but it seemed that his appeal had fallen on some selectively deaf ears. Drivers were known to have been working along the murder route – one even in the *Fairwater* pub car park immediately prior to Jack Armstrong's arrival there. 'They are certainly not helping us with our enquiries,' Superintendent Carsley bemoaned rather diplomatically at the time. Brook was to specifically lay the blame for the delay in finding Armstrong's body at the door of the other drivers whom he believed had hindered the establishment of the cab's route causing not only added distress to the family but the loss of vital hours in the pursuit of their suspect.

The anniversary of the killing in October 1980 would see what was in effect a repeat of the reconstruction of the murder drive along the A48. It appeared that the primary motivation for this was not so much to garner possible new leads but to reaffirm to the public that that the South Wales police had not forgotten Jack Armstrong nor his killer. An increasingly demoralised team of detectives faced with diminishing returns would see time sadly slip away and their investigation eventually scaled down to nearly nothing. For Viv Brook and his men their failure would be a personal nightmare. In his long career as head of South Wales CID up until the time of Armstrong's death, Brook had solved no less than 103 out of 106 murder cases over which he presided. They had met their nemesis in the mysterious Mr 'Williams'.

Reopening the case

The initial murder inquiry had been exhaustive. In its first year some 10,000 people had been interviewed in connection with the case and 2,000 written statements taken. Nearly 600 of those had been regarded as suspects – a number of those never formally eliminated. Although the crime would be re-examined in 1999, as part of a general review of South Wales 'unsolveds', and again more specifically in 2003, the case would remain unsolved. Jack's killer never identified; never found. For all these years it would seem that an exasperated South Wales police force had been chasing a ghost. Only weeks after the killing in 1979 an exasperated Detective Chief Superintendent Brooke somewhat prophetically proclaimed:

Somebody must have seen him; he can't have disappeared into thin air.

Retaining its original Art Deco style façade, the former offices of Armstrong's employers Castle Cabs has taken on a new life as a bar and restaurant. The author

But disappear he did, like a spectre – not into the darkest night but into a broad South Wales daylight. Strolling, as police would have it, along a busy thoroughfare and into the heart of a bustling village and complete anonymity.

Selected Sources

Newspapers and Journals
South Wales Echo (1887 to date)
Western Mail (1869 to date)
Glamorgan Gazette (1920–39)
Empire News & Sunday Chronicle (1954–60)
Cardiff & Merthyr Guardian (1845–50)
Cardiff & Suburban News (1952–64)
Cardiff Times (1858–1957)
Llandaff Parish Magazine (1977–78)
Humane Review (1908)
The Times (1840 to date)
Wales on Sunday (1989 to date)

Books and Directories
Western Mail (Kelly's) Directories (1880–1972)
Slater's Directory (1882–5)
Cardiff City Police annual reports (1914–68)
Cardiff Electoral Registers & Burgess Rolls (1875 to 1980)
The Illustrated History of Cardiff's Suburbs, Dennis Morgan (2003)
Cardiff: A history of the city, William Rees (1969)
Millennium Cardiff, John May (1999)
Seek out the Guilty, David Thomas (1969)
The Cardiff Book, Stewart Williams (editor), Vols. 1–3 (1973–77)
Descriptive catalogue of Madam D'Arc's Waxwork Exhibition,
    Victoria Rooms, St Mary Street Cardiff (1899)
Below the Bridge, Catherine Evans (1984)
Sailortown, Stan Hugill (1967)
Recollections reflections of a County policeman, W C May (1979)

Others
Cardiff Libraries' photographic collection
South Wales Constabulary Archives [and a special mention to all those too numerous to name who offered advice and snippets of information along the way, especially Mr Evans for his invaluable knowledge of Cardiff policing and crime detection].

Index

Personal names

Mahoney, Mrs 59, 61–63, 66
Marsden, Mr 62
Martin, Thomas 23
Matthews, Benjamin 26
Matthews, Charles 67
Medd, Hilda 96–98, 100–103
Medd, Irene 96, 98
Miles (St Mellons) 60, 63
Millman, Colonel 67
Mills, Hayley 139–140
Morgan, Brian 131
Morris, David 137
Morris, Reginald Oliver 96–103
Myerson, Aubrey 151

Naish, Ronald 137
Nathan, Francis 52
Norton family 56

O'Driscoll, Dr 103
Ohlsen, Andreas 38–40

Pearce, Mr 31
Perry, Mrs 51
Perry, William 45, 47–54
Phillips, Mr 80
Pittard, Marmaduke 87
Powell, Dr. Dennis 144
Pritchard, Mr 81
Pugsley, Detective Sergeant 98, 102

Reece, R L 23, 32, 49, 76, 91–92
Richards, John 20–22
Richards, Mr Justice 132
Richards, Rosie 100
Roberts Family (Llandaff) 147
Roberts, Mrs (Ely) 97, 101
Rowlands, John 68
Rutter, John 143

'S', Mrs 126
Sawyer, Mr 65
Scholberg, Dr. Harold 122
Scowcroft, Francis 87
Sennett, Margaret Winifred 135, 137, 140–144
Sennett, Paul Anthony 135
Shannon, Patrick 10
Sheen, Dr 50, 53
Sheppard, Inspector 64

Simpson, Patricia 137
Slater, Royston Churchill 143–144
Smith, William 73
Stacey, Harriet 83–86, *86*, 87–88, 90–93
Stacey, John 85–87, *87*, 89
Stockdale, Jeremiah Box 11, 23
Sullivan, Jack – see Thompson, John
Swann, Benjamin – see Jones, John
Sweetman, Mary Jane 81
Sweetman, Thomas (snr) 72, 76, 79, 81
Sweetman, Thomas ('Tommy') 73–76, *76*, 77–82

Temple-Morris, O 100, 102
Thomas, Police Superintendent 26
Thomas, John 77
Thompson, Annie 77
Thompson, John *75*, 75–77, 80
Thornton, Thomas 46–47, 51
Tissot, Mrs 57
Tomlinson, Reverend 56–57
Tudor, Gerald 117
Tull, John 109

Wallace, Dr 74
Wallace, Edgar 112
Warren, William Henry 86–89
Watkins, Judge Tasker 151–152
'Williams' (re: Jack Armstong investigation) 155, 157–158, 160–161, 164, 166
Williams, Mr (Grangetown) 92
Williams, Mr (Llanrumney Hall) 57
Williams, Mrs (Grangetown) 85, 88
Williams, Police Constable 32
Williams, David QC 151
Williams, John 22
Williams, Detective T 130
Williams, Thomas 36–37
'Wilson' (re: Ronald Lewis investigation) 126
Wilson, Chief Constable J A 107
Winton family 109
Wrenn, Phillip QC 143
Wulf, Captain C 38

Yelland, Inspector 87